The Boasted Advantages

Paul Henderson Scott

THE SALTIRE SOCIETY

The Boasted Advantages published 1999 by
The Saltire Society
9 Fountain Close,
22 High Street, Edinburgh EH1 1TF

A catalogue record for this book is available
from the British Library.

ISBN 0 85411 072 0

The Publishers acknowledge with thanks subsidy from the
Scottish Arts Council towards the publication of this volume.

Cover Design by James Hutcheson

Printed and bound in Scotland by Bell & Bain Limited

Contents

Other books by Paul Henderson Scott

1707: The Union of Scotland and England (1979)
Walter Scott and Scotland (1981)
John Galt (1985)
In Bed with an Elephant (1985)
The Thinking Nation (1989)
Cultural Independence (1989)
Towards Independence: Essays on Scotland (1991)
Andrew Fletcher and the Treaty of Union (1992)
Scotland in Europe: A Dialogue with a Sceptical Friend (1992)
Defoe in Edinburgh and Other Papers (1995)
A Mad God's Dream (1997)
Still in Bed with an Elephant (1998)

Edited

(with A.C. Davies) The Age of MacDiarmid (1980)
Sir Walter Scott's *The Letters of Malachi Malagrowther* (1981)
Andrew Fletcher's *United and Separate Parliaments* (1982)
(with George Bruce) A Scottish Postbag (1986)
(with A.C. Davies) Policy for the Arts: a selection
of AdCAS Papers (1991)
Scotland: A Concise Cultural History (1993)
(with Daniel Szechi) *Scotland's Ruine*: Lockhart of Carnwath's
Memoirs of the Union (1995)
(with Ian Gordon) John Galt's *The Member* and *The Radical* (1996)
Scotland: An Unwon Cause (1997)

Introduction

In his British Academy lecture in Edinburgh in November 1997 Neil MacCormick said that the Union of 1707 had been more often praised than studied.[1] He was echoing the thought of Robert Burns in his letter of 10 April 1790 to Mrs Dunlop. "Alas! have I often said to myself, what are all the boasted advantages which my country reaps from a certain Union, that can counterbalance the annihilation of her Independence, and even her very name." [2]

Burns' question was rhetorical, but it was one which still requires an answer. How did a Union which was forced on an unwilling Scotland and was vastly unpopular come to be regarded, as Gordon Donaldson said, "as part of the established and unalterable order of things?"[3] Donaldson thought that this was true of the period from about 1750 to about 1850 and that since then the Union has been increasingly challenged and criticised. Even so, there are still many people who appear to take it for granted that the Union is, and has always been, self-evidently beneficial, not only to England (which was its purpose) but also to Scotland. This belief is so firmly established in so many minds that politicians of three of our four main parties seem to be confident that they can argue for the preservation of the Union without having to explain why.

Now that the Scottish Parliament, in a limited form, is about to be restored after a century of effort, we now have to consider two constitutional options instead of three. Do we rest content with a Parliament with very restricted powers or do we move forward to the same status as any orther member state of the European Union, with our own international identity and name (to echo Burns again) and free in every respect from the control of London?

Whether or not the Union is beneficial to Scotland is therefore now the key question with immediate implications for our future.

The purpose of this book is to examine this question. Although the present and future must concern us most, they cannot be understood without some understanding of the past. In fact, this issue is hardly ever debated without some conscious or implied appeal to history. Unfortunately, as I hope to show, this appeal is usually to a false and untenable version of historical fact. Even the origin, purpose and nature of the Treaty are usually misrepresented. I therefore begin by an account of the historical background but I carry the story up to the present and to some reflections on our future prospects

P.H.S.
Edinburgh
June 1999

References

1   Neil MacCormick, text in Special Issue of *Scottish Affairs, Understanding Constitutional Change,* (Edinburgh 1998), p129.

2   Robert Burns, *Letters*, ed. J De Lancy Ferguson, (2 vols, Oxford, 1931), Vol II, p18.

3   Gordon Donaldson, in *Government and Nationalism in Scotland*, ed. J N Wolfe, (Edinburgh 1969), p4.

CHAPTER 1

Scotland before 1707

"One of the great success stories"

One of the persistent allegations of apologists for the Union is that Scotland in the centuries of independence before 1707 was more turbulent, impoverished and backward than other countries at comparable periods and that peace, prosperity and civilisation, everything that is desirable were all a consequence of the Union. This theory is so far from the truth that it was probably deliberately concocted as propaganda. A more charitable explanation is that it followed from an uncritical acceptance of the views of English historians. There was probably an element of both. In any case, it has been repeated so often that it is still widely believed.

The former Professor of Scottish History at Edinburgh University and Historiographer Royal, Gordon Donaldson, devoted one of his last public lectures in October 1989 to this point. He blamed the influence of English historians:

> Too much Scottish history which is being taught or absorbed today is still Scottish history as seen through English eyes, Scottish history interpreted from the English point of view. It is only right that every nation should have a proper pride in its own achievements, but the particular form which national conceit takes in England is the idea not only that English institutions have been and are superior to the institutions of all other countries, but also that in her historical development England was always far ahead of other countries. In English eyes anything that is not English is peculiar; worse that that, it is backward if not actually barbarous.

> The assumption that Scotland was backward can be challenged. We ought to have learned by this time that it is worthwhile at least trying to understand the institutions of Scotland instead of dismissing them as

unworthy of attention merely because they differ from those of England. It is not difficult to show that in many points Scotland was more mature in its outlook than England, was in many ways in advance of England, and thus to demonstrate that England was sometimes the backward country.[1]

Donaldson devoted the rest of his lecture to this demonstration. Other Scottish historians have recently said much the same. Alexander Grant, for instance, has pointed out that independent Scotland was a peaceful and stable country not only in comparison to England, but to Europe generally. "There is absolutely no evidence to support the idea of a continuous crown-nobility power struggle."[2] "Mediaeval Scotland was not conquered either by the Normans after 1066 or by Edward I and his successors after 1296; and it did not suffer nearly as many internal wars and violent power struggles as other mediaeval countries, especially England. It was one of the great success stories of the European middle ages."[3] Another historian, Fiona Watson, wrote recently: "I have every confidence that the Scots are more than capable of looking after themselves. After all, we managed it impressively well, despite perceptions to the contrary, up until 1603."[4] (1603 being the date, of course, when we effectively lost real independence.)

The success story was not only in stable and tolerant government, "rather a kindly place, and certainly a safer country to live in than many others," in Donaldson's words. [5] It was also outstanding in intellectual and artistic achievement, especially in poetry, philosophy, historiography, scholarship, music and architecture. Among the great names are the poets, William Dunbar, Robert Henryson, Gavin Douglas, David Lindsay, Alexander Scott, William Montgomery, George Buchanan; the philosophers, Duns Scotus and John Mair; the composer, Robert Carver; the mathematician, John Napier of Merchiston. Universities were founded in St. Andrews in 1411, Glasgow in 1451, Aberdeen in 1494 and Edinburgh in 1583. An Education Act of the Scottish Parliament of 1496 was the first legislation of its kind in Europe. Following John Knox's *First Book of Discipline* of 1560 a sustained effort was made by the Scottish Parliament to extend education to the whole population. It was in consequence of this, Lord Macaulay said in his *History of England* that "the common people of Scotland were superior in intelligence to the common people of any other country in Europe."[6]

These achievements were all the more remarkable because the south of Scotland, the wealthiest part of the country, was repeatedly laid waste by invading English armies. As the English historian, H.T. Buckle, wrote: "The darling object of the English, was to subjugate the Scotch; and if anything could increase the disgrace of so base an enterprise, it would have been that, having undertaken it, they ignominiously failed."[7] The suffering and loss caused by these attacks is beyond calculation; but paradoxically they also had a beneficial consequence. Scotland had to look elsewhere for friends and allies and found them on the continent of Europe. For centuries we had a close and fruitful association with other European countries, especially with France before the Reformation and with Holland afterwards. Scots were prominent as students and teachers in universities all over Europe. Between its foundation and the Reformation, the University of Paris had 17 or 18 Scottish Rectors.[8]

Dugald Stewart, who became Professor of Moral Philosophy in Edinburgh University in 1785, was widely regarded as one of the most brilliant university teachers of his generation. In one of his books he referred to the "constant influx of information and of liberality from abroad" which resulted from the continual intercourse "from time immemorial" between Scotland and the continent. He suggested that this might help to account for "the sudden burst of genius, which to a foreigner must seem to have sprung up in this country by a sort of enchantment, soon after the Rebellion of 1745."[9] He was referring to what we now call the Scottish Enlightenment, a period when Scotland was alive with innovative ideas in philosophy, economics, sociology, geology, chemistry, agriculture, engineering and much else. An American, Harold Thompson, said that "to discover comparable achievements by so small a nation in so short a time we should need to go back ... to the age of Pericles."[10] Perhaps he should have said to the age of Renaissance Florence; but certainly the Scottish Enlightenment was one of the great periods of intellectual energy.

There was, of course, no sudden enchantment about it. Such a confident outpouring of new ideas by so many people in so many disciplines needed a solid basis of generations of scholarship. Scotland was not only constantly in touch with the rest of Europe, but had a strong tradition in philosophy and history since at least the 14th century.[11] Scots had been at the leading edge of innovative thought more than once before the 18th century. Metaphysical speculation and rational analysis were encouraged by the intellectual traditions of the Reformed Kirk. As John MacQueen has said, "the Scottish Enlightenment was the natural, almost the inevitable outcome of several centuries of Scottish and European intellectual history."[12]

The most outrageous and absurd claim made by the apologists for the Union is that the Scottish Enlightenment derived from it, under the stimulus of influence from England. Such a deep-rooted and diverse intellectual movement could not have been created out of nothing in about forty years. In any case, England was not strong in innovative thought in the early 18th century. This claim is part of the attempt to denigrate the Scottish past by suggesting that all good things come from England by courtesy of the Union. Frantz Fanon, Michael Hechter and others have argued that colonial powers must denigrate the culture of dependent territories to justify their domination and undermine the will to resist and that they achieve this with the voluntary co-operation of assimilated élites within the colonised territory.[13] Whether or not one accepts that Scotland has, in effect, been a colony of England since 1707, there is no doubt that a denigration of Scottish culture has been one of the consequences of the Union.

I do not suggest that this policy has been deliberately planned or intended. It has happened almost as an automatic result of the political domination of Scotland by one of the most self-confident and successful powers in the world, as England was between the Battle of Waterloo and the Second World War. In his *Letters of Malachi Malagrowther* Sir Walter Scott (making a similar point to Gordon Donaldson in the passage which I quoted) said that, "The English act on the principle that everything English is right and that anything in Scotland which is not English must therefore be wrong."[14] Since they are much more numerous than us and since most of the levers of wealth, power and propaganda are in their hands, many people in Scotland have tended to accept their judgement. Hence the assimilated élite. Hence too the fact that Scottish education has for a long period tended to concentrate more on English literature, history, conditions and ideas than on anything Scottish.

This is the reason why *A Claim of Right for Scotland* of July 1988 (the report from which the Constitutional Convention and the Scotland Act derive) said: "The Union has always been, and remains, a threat to the survival of a distinctive culture in Scotland."[15] I think that it is even more serious than that. Generations of Scots have left school knowing almost nothing about their own country and with the impression that everything of any importance always happens somewhere else. This is a recipe for a massive inferiority complex, even self-hatred, and an expectation of failure. A happy and satisfactory society is hardly possible in these circumstances.

References

1   Gordon Donaldson, 'A Backward Nation?' in *Scotland's History*, ed. James Kirk, (Edinburgh 1995), p43.

2   Alexander Grant, *Independence and Nationhood*, Vol. III of *The New History of Scotland* (London 1984), p172.

3   Alexander Grant, 'The Middle Ages: the Defence of Independence' in *Why Scottish History Matters*, ed. Rosalind Mitchison, (Edinburgh, 1997), pp31,39.

4   Fiona Watson in *Scotland On Sunday*, 25th January 1998.

5   Gordon Donaldson, op.cit., p46.

6   Thomas Babington Macaulay, *History of England*, (London 1858), Vol.IV, pp782-3.

7   Henry Thomas Buckle, '*On Scotland and the Scotch Intellect*' in *History of Civilisation*, (1857 and 1861), ed. H J Hanham, (Chicago 1970), p31.

8   Alexander Broadie, *The Tradition of Scottish Philosophy*, (Edinburgh 1990), p3.

9   Dugald Stewart, *Collected Works*, ed. Sir William Hamilton, 2 volumes, Vol. I (Edinburgh 1854-60), p550-1.

10 Harold W Thompson, *Henry Mackenzie: A Scottish Man of Feeling*, (Edinburgh 1931), p1.

11 Alexander Broadie *op.cit.*, and David Allan, *Virtue, Learning and the Scottish Enlightenment*, (Edinburgh 1993), p9 and passim.

12 John MacQueen, *Progress and Poetry: The Enlightenment and Scottish Literature* (Edinburgh 1982), p5.

13 Michael Hechter, *Internal Colonialism* (London 1975), pp73, 81.

14 Sir Walter Scott, *The Letters of Malachi Malagrowther* (1826), ed. P H Scott (Edinburgh 1981), p9.

15 *A Claim of Right for Scotland: Report of the Constitutional Steering Committee*, (Edinburgh 1988), para 2.2, p2.

CHAPTER 2

The Road to Union

Saint-Simon in his *Memoirs* recorded the reaction of the Court of Louis XIV to the news of the Treaty of Union:

> It passes understanding how so proud a nation, hating the English, well-acquainted with them through past sufferings and moreover so jealous of their own freedom and independence should have submitted to bow their necks beneath such a yoke.[1]

This was a very natural comment. The Scots had successfully defended their independence against very heavy odds for centuries. Why had they now surrendered without any apparent struggle? It was not because of any change in the attitude of the two countries to one another. In the words of the English historian, J. A. Froude, "the English hated Scotland because Scotland had successfully defied them: the Scots hated England as an enemy on the watch to make them slaves."[2] Daniel Defoe at the beginning of his *History of the Union* said, "Never two nations, that had so much affinity in circumstances, have had such inveteracy and aversion to one another in their blood."[3] In such an atmosphere, it seems unexpected and improbable that England should at last obtain their objective by political and not military means.

The events which led to this outcome began with the marriage in 1503 of James IV to Margaret Tudor, the daughter of the English King, Henry VII. James had sought this marriage in the hope of securing an enduring peace with England. This hope was disappointed because only ten years later Scotland suffered the disastrous defeat at Flodden when James himself was killed. Even so, his great-grandson, James VI, by virtue of his descent from Margaret Tudor, succeeeded also to the English throne in 1603 as James I. That this was a possible outcome had been foreseen in the English Court when

Margaret Tudor's marriage was under consideration:

> Some of Henry's advisers ... disliked the project. They saw, just as clearly
> as James did, that it might bring England under the rule of a Scottish
> prince. Henry reassured them. If such a union took place, he argued, it
> would be an accession, not of England to Scotland, but of Scotland to
> England, since the greater would always draw the less, as England had
> drawn Normandy under her sway. [4]

Henry was right. In the 17th century the monarch, both in Scotland
and England, was still the effective head of the executive arm of
government. When James VI moved south to London, Scotland
remained nominally independent and still had its own Parliament,
but it was under the remote control of a monarch, surrounded by
English ministers, who had to give precedence to English interests.
In Defoe's words, "Scotland was after this in a political though not
in a legal sense, always under the management of the English court
... It had the subjection without the advantages."[5] Since foreign
policy was among the royal prerogatives, Scotland ceased to have
a foreign policy and a recognisable international identity. P. F.
Tytler ends his *History of Scotland* with a melancholy account of the
gloomy feelings of the people as James left Scotland, which then
ceased in effect to be a separate and independent Kingdom.[6] Or, as a
more recent historian, Hume Brown, said:

> The Union of the Crowns brought many disadvantages to Scotland, but
> the result of it that most vitally affected her was her severance from the
> nations at a period when new principles and new ideas were guiding
> their policy. Throughout the entire 17th century Scotland was a severed
> and withered branch, and her people knew it.[7]

In consequence of the Union of the Crowns, the history of Scotland
in the 17th century is largely one of decline. The civil wars were
provoked by the interference of James VI and Charles I in the affairs
of the church which they would hardly have attempted if they had
remained in Scotland. They led to the humiliation of the Cromwellian

occupation. During most of the century Scottish trade was damaged by England's wars against our traditional trading partners. Since the making of war and peace was also a royal prerogative, Scotland was obliged to supply men and money for these wars, but was forgotten in the peace settlements and was left virtually defenceless at home.

After James VII and II fled in 1688, the Scottish Parliament adopted a Claim of Right which deposed him from the Scottish throne and offered it to William and Mary on condition that Parliament had "freedom of speech and debate." This was an improvement, but there was still a joint monarchy which left all state appointments in royal hands and Acts of Parliament were still subject to royal assent. This semi-independence rapidly became intolerable. The last straw was the failure of the Darien Scheme, an attempt to establish a trading colony in the Isthmus of Panama, in which many people in Scotland had invested most of their disposable wealth. William, as King of Scotland, had approved the Act establishing the company; but, as King of England, had done his best to sabotage it.

A new Parliament, which met for the first time in 1703, concentrated on finding a solution to the weakness of Scotland's position under the joint monarchy. They were presented with an opportunity to escape from it. The last surviving child of Queen Anne had died in July 1700 and there was then no obvious successor to the throne. The English Parliament, without consulting Scotland, passed the Act of Succession of 1701 which offered it to the Electress of Hanover and her descendants. This was in no sense binding on Scotland and the Scottish Parliament therefore proceeded to consider the Scottish succession.

Andrew Fletcher of Saltoun, known since his own time as "the Patriot", took a leading role in the debate. He described the consequences of the joint monarchy:

> All our affairs since the union of the crowns have been managed by the advice of English ministers, and the principal offices of the kingdom filled with such men, as the court of England knew would be subservient

to their designs...We all know that this is the cause of our poverty, misery and dependence ... So that there is no way to free this country from a ruinous dependence upon the English court, unless by placing the power of conferring offices and pensions in the Parliament, so long as we shall have the same King with England.[8]

Fletcher therefore proposed that, on the death of Queen Anne, Parliament should decide on a royal succession different from the English or legislate to transfer all power from the monarchy to Parliament itself. This proposal was embodied in the Act of Security passed in July 1703. Royal assent was refused and so Parliament passed the same Act again in the following year. This time the assent was given, but the English Parliament now reacted to this attempt by the Scottish Parliament to assert independence and escape from London control. Both the Commons and the Lords in England adopted an Act, usually called the Aliens Act, "for the effectual securing the Kingdom of England from the apparent dangers that may arise from several Acts lately passed by the Parliament of Scotland." The first part called for the appointment by the Queen of commissioners to "treat and consult" with Scottish commissioners "concerning the union of the two Kingdoms." The second part was much more aggressive and threatened sanctions against Scotland if the Scots had not accepted the same royal succession as England by 25th December, 1705. If they failed to do this, all Scots would be treated in England as aliens and incapable of inheriting property and the import from Scotland of cattle and other main articles of trade would be banned.

It is significant that the trigger for the application of these sanctions was not agreement to negotiate but the acceptance of the same royal sucession. Since 1603 it had been the means by which the English Government had controlled Scotland and they did not intend to relinquish it without a struggle. The proposal for negotiations about union looked like a conciliatory gesture. At that time the word, union, did not have the significance of incorporation which it acquired with the Treaty of 1707. The examples of usage before that date in the Oxford English Dictionary show that it was generally used to mean an association or alliance for any common purpose or the mere absence of dissension or discord. There were many outstanding matters between the two countries which the Scots would have been happy to discuss. When it came to the point, the English made their intentions clear by speaking about an "incorporating" union.

Scotland was at this time in a very weak bargaining position. The joint monarchy had left the country with virtually no defence forces. England had a strong army, experienced in continental wars, under Marlborough, one of the most successful military commanders of the period in Europe. Scotland's foreign trade had been damaged by the wars fought in the interests of England. The propertied classes had lost their savings in the Darien scheme. To make matters worse, there had been a succession of years of bad weather and poor harvests.

Scotland was also in a weak position politically. Not only were the ministers in the Scottish Goverment appointed, paid and instructed by London, but other members of Parliament were also paid for their support. Some recent historians have argued that we should not be shocked by this because it was the normal practice of the time; but the effort made to secure the acceptance of the Treaty of Union by the Scottish Parliament was on a completely exceptional scale. Even the Duke of Hamilton, who professed to lead the opposition and was therefore cheered whenever he appeared on the streets of Edinburgh, was in the pay of the English Government. Several times at crucial stages during the three-months-long debate on the Treaty he frustrated and undermined his own side. The most damaging of all was even before the negotation. He contrived a Parliamentary ambush which resulted in a vote which left the appointment of the Scottish commissioners to the Queen. Shortly afterwards he wrote to his English contact: "I have done her Majesty signal service."[9] This meant that no real negotiation was now possible. Both teams of commissioners were appointed by the English Government and were men on whom they could rely. There was only one exception, George Lockhart of Carnwath, who was included because he had a family connection with the influential English Whig, Lord Wharton. This had the advantage that Lockhart was afterwards able to give a first hand account in his admirably vivid *Memoirs*, which are one of the best sources for the period.[10]

When the Scottish commissioners arrived in London, it was made clear to them from the start that they had very little freedom of manoeuvre. The English insisted on considering only their own proposal for an "incorporating" union, an appropriate name because it meant in effect the absorption of the Scottish Parliament as a small minority within the English one. The Scottish Secretary of State, the Earl of Mar, wrote to a colleague in Edinburgh: "You see what we are to treat of is not in our choice, and that we see the inconveniences of treating an incorporating union only."[11] There were hardly any meetings between the two sides, even, as one said, "to drink a glass of wine."[12] The business was conducted by the exchange of notes, except once when the Scots insisted on a meeting to protest about the small numbers of members they were to be allowed in the two Houses of Parliament.[13]

One of the Scottish commissioners, Sir John Clerk of Penicuik, afterwards wrote a history of the transaction, in the discreet obscurity of Latin, in which he was blunt about the political realities. He said in this that as soon as Scotland began to assert a desire for independence, as in the Act of Security, it became a "necesary policy" for the English Government "either to destroy us or to force us into a union on well-defined terms." The Scottish commissioners had no choice: "You cannot force your will on those stronger than yourself." In a testament which he left for his family and friends as a justification for his support for the Union he said that the alternative was invasion by England. Since their population was at least four times more numerous, they would have found "little or no difficulty in subdueing us ... and in treating us ignominiously & cruelly as a conquered province."[14]

From the English point of view, it was a vital national interest to keep control of Scotland because England was engaged in a long, intermittent war with France, Scotland's ancient ally. The English Government saw a risk that an independent Scotland might once again ally herself with France. The purpose of the Union of 1707 was not to serve Scotland but to keep it under control in the strategic interest of England. This was such an important objective for the English Government that they mounted a remarkably determined, sophisticated and skilful operation to achieve it, involving military intimidation, propaganda, secret agents, bribery and inducements in the articles of the Treaty itself to the members of the Scottish Parliament. It was easy enough for them to get the agreement of the Scottish commissioners; the consent of the Scottish Parliament, which had asserted independence so robustly in 1703 and 1704, was more difficult and uncertain. Although, as Clerk said, the Scots knew that they were acting under the threat of invasion, the English were subtle enough most of the time, to let this speak for itself. The English Lord Treasurer, the Chief Minister of the government the Earl of Godolphin, sent a polite but menacing letter to the Scottish Chancellor, the Earl of Seafield, in July 1703:

England is now in war with France; if Scotland were in peace, and consequently at liberty to trade with France, would that not immediately necessitate a war betwixt England and Scotland also, as has often been the case before the two nations were under the same sovereign? And though perhaps some turbulent spirits in Scotland may be desiring to have it so again, if they please to consult history they will not find the advantage of those breaches has often been on the side of Scotland; and if they give themselves leave to consider how much England is increased in wealth and power since those times, perhaps the present conjuncture will not appear more favourable for them, but on the contrary rather furnish arguments for enforcing the necessity of a speedy union between the two nations; which is a notion that I am sorry to find has so little prevalency in the present parliament of Scotland, and I hope your lordship will not be offended with me if I take the freedom to be of opinion they may possibly be sorry for it too, when the opportunity is out of their reach.[15]

During the debate in the Scottish Parliament, the English Government, acting on the advice of Marlborough, moved infantry and cavalry to the border. Sir David Nairne, the Deputy Secretary for Scottish Affairs in Whitehall, wrote to Mar about them on 20th November 1706: "They have the necessary orders; but all relateing to this affair must be kept very private."[16]

Daniel Defoe was the most celebrated, but not the only, secret agent employed to report on developments in Edinburgh and to ingratiate himself with Scottish politicians and try to influence them. As a propagandist he was tireless. His newsletter, *The Review*, appeared three times a week and for two years it was dominated by arguments for the Union. He wrote at least eight pamphlets on the subject, all of them anonymously, and in two of them pretended to be a Scot advising his fellow countrymen. In his *History of the Union*, he too was frank about invasion as the alternative to Scottish acceptance of the Treaty. There was, he wrote, no other way left, to prevent the most bloody war that ever had been between the two nations."[17]

Bribery of members of the Scottish Parliament was on such a scale that it became legendary. Hence Robert Burns:

> We're bought and sold for English gold,
> Such a parcel of rogues in a nation! [18]

In the whole of the 19th century the most frank account of the Union transaction was in Sir Walter Scott's *Tales of a Grandfather*. He too had strong words about bribery:

The distribution of this money constituted the charm by which refractory Scottish members were reconciled to the Union. The interests of Scotland were considerably neglected in the Treaty of Union; and in consequence, the nation instead of regarding it as an identification of the interests of both Kingdoms, considered it as a total surrender of their independence, by their false and corrupted statesmen ... despised by the English and detested by their own country.[19]

There is overwhelming evidence of bribery in the surviving corespondence. To give only one example, the Earls of Seafield and Glasgow wrote on 20th July 1707 to the Duke of Queensberry, the Lord Commissioner in the session of the Scottish Parliament which approved the Union. Glasgow was in charge of the distribution of £20,000, a substantial sum at that time, received from Godolphin, the English Lord Treasurer to ease the passage of the Union. Queensberry had asked for an account of the distribution which he could produce to Godolphin. In their joint reply Seafield and Glasgow said:

> It is impossible to state these soumes without discovering this haill affair to every particular person that received any part of the money, which hath been hitherto keeped secret, and it is more than probable, that they would refuse to give a signatory if they were demanded of them, so the discovery of it would be of no use, unless it were to bring discredit upon the management of that parliament.

The letter ends with the note: "Your Grace may be pleased to burn this letter when you have read it to my Lord Treasurer".[20] But Godolphin evidently insisted prudently on retaining the letter. It remained in his family until it was sold to the British Museum in 1892.

The secret was not kept for long. After the Union, Lockhart of Carnwath was elected to the new British Parliament and in 1711 became a member of a parliamentary Commission to examine the public accounts. Under oath, Glasgow produced a list of those who had shared in the £20,000. They ranged from £12,325 to the Duke of Queensberry, £1,104 to the Earl of Marchmont, £1,000 each to the Duke of Athol and the Marquis of Tweedale to a mere £11 to Lord Bamf.[21] Sir Walter Scott commented: "It may be doubted whether the descendants of the noble lords and honourable gentlemen who accepted this gratification would be more shocked at the general fact of their ancestors being corrupted, or scandalised at the paltry amount of the bribe."[22] There are 32 names, mostly peers, in the list; the Treaty was finally ratified by a majority of 41.

More subtle inducements than the straightforward payments of money were included in the Treaty. Several of the clauses were direct appeals to the self-interest of the classes represented in Parliament. To the lords, the continuation of their heritable jurisdictions and the grant of the rights of English peers (although only 16 of them would sit in the House of Lords); to the commissioners of the burghs, the guarantee of their rights and privileges; to the lawyers, the guarantee that the Scottish legal system would continue. The resistance of the Church was overcome by a separate but associated Act which guaranteed that the Church of Scotland was "to continue without any alteration to the people of this land in all succeeding generations." Above all there was the ingenious Equivalent, a payment to Scotland of £398,085. 10 shillings which was supposed to serve several purposes simultaneously. It was to be compensation to Scotland for accepting a share of the English National Debt and agreeing to the abolition of the Darien company. It was to be used to encourage manufactures and fisheries; but the first call on it was to repay the capital of the investors in the Darien scheme along with accumulated interest. Since many members of the Scottish Parliament and their families and friends thought that they had lost their savings in that venture, this was a powerful persuader. But that was not the end of the ingenuity of the drafters of the Treaty. The Equivalent was to be paid by Scotland through an increse in Excise Duty. "In fact", Sir Walter Scott said, "the Parliamentof Scotland was bribed with public monies belonging to their own country. In this way, Scotland herself was made to pay the price given to her legislators for the sacrifice of her independence."[23]

Every contemporary source agrees that the Treaty was detested by the great majority of the Scottish people. Petitions against it, and none in favour, flooded into Parliament. Sir John Clerk, who tried hard in his *History* and other writings to justify his part in achieving the Union, said that "not even one per cent approved."[24] Why then did a majority in Parliament agree to it? With one or two exceptions, they were the same men who had asserted Scottish independence by voting by a large majority for the Act of Security in 1703 and 1704. A substantial number of them had therefore changed their minds or at least their votes. As we have seen, Clerk's explanation was a belief that the only alternative to the Treaty was invasion and the imposition of worse terms, but he was looking for a respectable excuse. Scottish opinion seems to have had little doubt that English gold was the real cause. From about the middle of the 19th century a belief began to establish itself that the Scots had exchanged their independence for access to English and colonial trade, but I shall discuss this in the next chapter.

Under the terms of the Treaty, the two Kingdoms of Scotland and England were to be united into one Kingdom to be known as Great Britain with the same Hanoverian succession and with one and the same Parliament of Great Britain. In this new Parliament, Scotland was to have 45 members in the Commons and 16 in the Lords, less than 10% of the total, and therefore too small a minority to have much influence. There was no provision for arbitration over any disputes that might arise or to allow for amendmends. The arrangements were clearly intended to be permanent. Scotland had been reduced to political impotence and placed under English control.

The advantages to England of the Treaty were obvious. The possibility of a Jacobite restoration had been greatly reduced. Scotland could no longer take a separate monarch and ally herself with France. England had secured her northern frontier and could pursue her ambitions in Europe and beyond without having to keep a watch on the north. It secured new sources of men for the forces, of revenues for the customs and a safe market for English manufactures. The Union was a bloodless annexation of Scotland to England, the satisfaction of a centuries-old ambition, achieved at little cost, and leaving England's institutions, coinage, weights and measures and everything else unchanged. The Scottish Parliament was abolished. In spite of the language of the Treaty, the English Parliament continued as before, without even the formality of a new election, apart from the addition of the few Scottish members.

Scotland now had only the guarantees contained in the Treaty. In one of his pamphlets before Defoe argued that the Scots could now have complete confidence that the guarantees were sacrosanct. Since the Treaty was the foundation of the new Parliament, no article of the Treaty could be violated without the Parliament dissolving itself.[25] I do not know if Defoe believed his own propaganda (although I doubt it), but others at the time took a more realistic view. Gilbert Burnet in *His History of His Own Time* said, "where a supreme legislature is once acknowledged, nothing can be unalterable." When he first had news of the Treaty, Robert Wodrow in a letter of 30 May 1706 expressed his reaction:

> I have a great many melancholy thoughts of living to see this ancient Kingdome made a province, and not only our religiouse and civil liberty lost, but lost irrevocably, and this is the most dismall aspect ane incorporating union has to me, that it putts matters past help. Though many a time we have been over run and our civil and religious rights invaded, yet at the next turn we had them restored some way, as 1572, 1638, 1688. But now, once lost, ever lost.

Or, as the Speaker of the House of Commons said, "We have catched Scotland and will not let her go."[26] It is easy to understand the rage and frustration of Andrew Fletcher who had struggled so hard to defend Scottish independence. It is said that he left Parliament House after the final vote on the Treaty with the bitter words that Scotland was now only fit for the slaves who had sold it. His nephew recorded that as he lay dying in 1716 almost his last words were, "Lord have mercy on my poor country that is barbarously oppressed."[27]

The English Parliament, thus transformed in 1707 into the British Parliament, has always behaved as the English Parliament continuing. One sign of this is that the Treaty of Union is almost invariably referred to in England as the Act (in the singular) of Union, as if it were an ordinary Act of Parliament, and not the legal basis of its existence, in the Defoe theory at least. The Scottish institutions guaranteed in the Treaty (that is the legal system, the Church, the local administration and the education system which was originally dependent on the last two of these) have remained to some extent distinct; but the British Parliament has had little inhibition in passing legislation which affects them or in other ways disregarding the provisions of the Treaty. This began almost as soon as the Treaty came into force. It imposed, for example, the English treason law on Scotland in 1709 and lay patronage on the Church of Scotland in 1712. By 1713 even the Scots, such as Mar and Seafield, who had helped to accomplish the Treaty were so disillusioned with it that they moved for its repeal in the House of Lords and failed by only four votes.

References

1   Duc de Saint-Simon, *Memoirs* (41 volumes, Paris 1901), *quoted* by John S Gibson in *Playing the Scottish Card: The Jacobite Invasion of 1708* (Edinburgh 1988), p103.

2   James A Froude, *History of England*, (London 1873), Vol. IV, p5.

3   Daniel Defoe, *History of the Union*, (Edition of 1786, London), p37.

4   Polydor Vergil, *Historia Anglica*, Vol. II, pp153-40; *quoted* in R L Mackie, *King James IV of Scotland*, (Edinburgh 1958), p93.

5   Daniel Defoe, op.cit., p50.

6   P F Tytler, *History of Scotland* (Edinburgh, 1864), Vol. IV p316.

7   P Hume Brown, *The Union of 1707* (Glasgow 1907), p4.

8   Andrew Fletcher of Saltoun, Speech to the Scottish Parliament, 1703, in *Selected Political Writings and Speeches of Andrew Fletcher of Saltoun*, ed. David Daiches (Edinburgh 1979), pp70-1.

[9]   See Paul H Scott, *Andrew Fletcher and the Treaty of Union,* (Edinburgh 1992 and 1994), p142 and passim.

[10]   George Lockhart of Carnwath. A modern edition of his *Memoirs,* ed. Daniel Szechi with a Foreword by Paul H. Scott, has been published as *'Scotland's Ruine': Lockhart of Carnwath's Memoirs of the Union* (Aberdeen 1995).

[11]   Earl of Mar in *State Papers and Letters Addressed to William Carstares,* ed. by Joseph McCormick, (Edinburgh 1774), pp743-4.

[12]   James Erskine in a letter to the Earl of Mar in *Report on the Manuscripts of the Earl of Mar and Kellie* (HMC, London 1904), p271.

[13]   Sir John Clerk of Penicuik, *History of the Union of Scotland and England,* translated and edited by Douglas Duncan, (Edinburgh SHS 1993) p85, fn2.

[14]   *Ibid.* pp162,173,186.

[15]   Historical Manuscripts Commission, Report XIV, Appendix Part III, p198; *quoted* in P H Scott, *1707: The Union of Scotland and England* (Edinburgh 1979), p47.

[16]   Report on the Manuscripts of the Earl of Mar and Kellie (HMC, London 1904), pp336,353.

[17]   Defoe, *op. cit.,* p64.

[18]   Robert Burns, 'Such a Parcel of Rogues in a Nation' in *Poems and Songs,* ed. James Kinsley, (London 1969), pp511-2 and other editions.

[19]   Sir Walter Scott, *Tales of a Grandfather,* edition of 1889, pp749, 768,754,770.

[20]   British Library, Add. MSS 34,180; quoted in P H Scott, *1707: The Union of Scotland and England, op. cit.,* pp43-4.

[21]   George Lockhart, *op. cit.,* p.257.

[22]   Sir Walter Scott, *op. cit.,* p769.

[23]   *Ibid.* p769.

[24]   Sir John Clerk, *op.cit.,* p118

[25]   Daniel Defoe, *A Fourth Essay at Removing National Prejudices* (London 1706), p26.

[26]   Robert Woodrow, *Early Letters, ed.* L W Sharp, (Edinburgh 1937), p291.

[27]   Andrew Fletcher of Saltoun, 'Letters' in Scottish History Society, *Miscellany X,* (Edinburgh 1965), p171.

CHAPTER 3

Was the Union a Bargain over Trade?

P. W. J. Riley's book, *The Union of England and Scotland* (1978) is the most thorough study which exists of the Union from an English point of view. He concludes that "Trade was hardly more than a propaganda argument for embracing or opposing a union designed for quite other reasons". And again, "Contrary to an apparently reasonable hypothesis, trade considerations seem to have exerted no influence worth speaking of."[1] I have studied the same questions from the other side for at least 20 years and, on this point, I entirely agree with Riley. It has been argued since about the middle of the last century that the Union was a freely negotiated bargain which Scotland traded her independence for access to the markets of England and the Plantations (as the colonies were then called). We have already seen that it was not a free bargain of any kind. The idea that trade was a major factor also fails to stand up to an examination of the evidence.

Eventually, the Union certainly affected Scottish trade in many ways, some beneficial and some adverse. That is a separate question from the one at issue, although some recent writers have confused the two. The present question is not one about conseqences, but about causes. Were considerations of trade a major motive either in the acceptance of the Treaty by the Scottish commissioners or in the votes in the Scottish Parliament?

The idea that trade was a major motive behind the Union can be traced to a correspondence between two distinguished historians in the 1850s. Thomas Babington Macaulay was writing his *History of England* when he wrote to Hill Burton, the author of an 8-volume *History of Scotland*. Macaulay said that as he approached the period of the Union he saw some points of difficulty: "One was that although the Union was notoriously unpopular in Scotland, yet there were symptoms of pressure on the side of Scotland in its direction." In his reply Burton suggested that "he would find a simple solution in the urgency of the Scots for participation in the English trade". Macaulay wrote back on 20th November 1852 to say that he thought that this was "quite right".[2]

This "simple solution" was taken up so eagerly by some historians and unionist politicians that it became widely accepted as though it were an undoubted fact. There were several reasons, I think, why the theory was attractive. In the first place, many people were puzzled by the Union and felt a need to find a plausible explanation for the sudden abandonment by the Scottish Parliament of the independence which the Scots had fought so long and so heroically to defend. Also, especially if they wanted to make a case for the Union, they were reluctant to face the unpalatable fact that it was imposed on Scotland by intimidation and bribery. As Hume Brown said, "A people does not gladly turn its eyes to a period when its representative men whether from their own natural failings or as the result of temporary circumstances, compromise the national character in the eyes of the world."[3] The facts were unflattering to both England and Scotland; one was revealed as a bully and the other as the victim who not only tamely surrendered but was corrupted forby. The new explanation apparently looked less damaging to both parties. It may be doubted whether it is more respectable to surrender independence for trading advantages than to avoid invasion, but the theory about trade did at least imply that there was a rational bargain with benefits to both sides. This met the needs of both self-esteem and of propaganda, even if it disregarded the historical evidence.

Of the "symptoms of pressure", which Macaulay mentioned, one of the most often quoted is in a letter from the Earl of Roxburgh of 28th November 1705:

The motives will be, Trade with most, Hanover with some, ease and security with others, together with a general aversion at civill discords, intollerable poverty, and the general oppression of a bad ministry, from generation to generation, without the least regard to the good of the country.

"Trade with most" sounds decisive enough, but it was an isolated remark. Roxburgh was one of the leaders of a floating group in the Scottish Parliament known as the Squadrone Volante. They had at first supported Fletcher but afterwards switched to support for the Union apparently in return for a promise, which was not kept, that they would be put in charge of the distribution of the Equivalent. When this letter was written Roxburgh was agonising over this change of policy. In his letters he veers about between almost every possible point of view. He says, for instance, that the Treaty "is destruction for Scotland" and elsewhere that the alternative to Succession or a Union was military conquest by England "upon the first peace", by which he meant as soon as Marlborough's army was disengaged in Europe.[4] During the debate on the Treaty, Seton of Pitmedden used the argument about trade. He too had originally supported Fletcher; but he sold his services to the Government for a pension of £100 a year.

There was a significant episode during the debate on the Act of Security in 1703, when the Government attempted to use an offer of access to English and colonial trade as an alternative to the clause which was a clear declaration of independence. This clause stated that Scotland would not choose the same succession to the Scottish throne as England unless "there be such conditions of government settled and enacted as may secure the honour and independency of the Crown of this Kingdom, the freedom, frequency and power of the parliament, and the religion, liberty and trade of the Nation from the English or any foreign influence." The Lord Advocate proposed instead that the clause following "unless" should read: "a free communication of trade, the freedom of Navigation and the liberty of the Plantations be fully agreed and established by the Parliament and Kingdom of England in favour of the subjects and Kingdom of Scotland."[5] Parliament had no objection to this, but evidently did not regard it as an adequate substitute. So they simply frustrated the Government's attempt at diversion by adopting both clauses. When the same Act eventually received royal assent in the following year, the Lord Advocate's clause was omitted. This produced no reaction in Scotland and no mention in Parliament. Evidently, the offer of access to the English and colonial trade was not regarded at the time as a major issue.

Andrew Fletcher commented on the Lord Advocate's intervention in a pamphlet which he wrote after the parliamentary session of 1703. This was the most important of his publications, *An Account of a Conversation Concerning a Right Regulation of Government for the Common Good of Mankind.* It is in the form of a report of a discussion, presumably imaginary, in London and between Fletcher himself, two English Members of Parliament and the Earl of Cromarty (who was the one undoubted Scottish enthusiast for an incorporating union.) Cromarty raises the subject of the Lord Advocate's clause:

> But sure you will allow, said the Earl, that a free commerce with England, and the liberty of trading to their plantations, which cannot be expected without a union, must be of incomparable advantage to the Scots nation, unless you will disown one of your darling clauses in the act of security.

Fletcher at an earlier part of the conversation argued that a union, because of English competition, "would certainly destroy even those manufactures we now have." He replies to Cromarty:

> My lord, said I, the clause you mean is placed there without the condition of a union; and your lordship cannot forget, was brought in by the court as an equivalent of all limitations, and in order to throw out another clause, which declares that we would not nominate the same successor with England, unless sufficient limitations were first enacted. This was done to mislead the commissioners of burghs, who for the most part are for anything that bears the name of trade, though but a sham, as this was. And nothing could be more just than to turn it upon the court by adding both clauses; which sunk your party in the house for a long time after.

For my own part, I cannot see what advantage a free trade to the English plantations would bring us, except a farther exhausting of our people, and the utter ruin of all our merchants, who should vainly pretend to carry that trade from the English ... I desired him to consider that Wales, the only country that ever had united with England, lying at a less distance from London, and conseqently more commodiously to participate in the circulation of a great trade than we do, after three or four hundred years, is still the only place of that kingdom, which has no considerable commerce, though possessed of one of the best ports in the whole island; a sufficient demonstration that trade is not a necessary consequence of a union with England.[6]

The royal burghs, which were responsible for foreign trade, were opposed to the Union and were one of the great number of bodies who petitioned Parliament against it. They argued that Scottish trade would be damaged by the imposition of taxes designed to meet English conditions and because "all the concerns of trade and other interests" would be subject to "such alterations as the Parliament of Great Britain shall think fit."[7]

They were right. The immediate effect of the Union was harmful to the Scottish economy and it took several decades to recover. In his pamphlets before the ratification of the Treaty Defoe argued that it would bring trading advantages to Scotland. Twenty years later, when he made a tour through Scotland, he admitted that he had been wrong. In his account of his journey he said that there had been no increase of trade and population since the Union, "but rather the contrary" and that the people were not only poor, but looked poor. [8]

No one was in a better position to know the facts about this than Sir John Clerk, who was concerned with financial and trade questions both as a commissioner for the Treaty and as a Baron of the Exchequer afterwards. He was also anxious in his various writings on the subject to justify the Treaty and his own part in it. He does not suggest that it was a bargain over trade and does not claim that it had beneficial economic consequences. In a paper which he wrote in 1730 about "the present circumstances of Scotland", the most that he could say was that "things had not really got much worse but remained on balance very much the same."[9]

By 1760 Adam Smith (for reasons which I shall consider in the next chapter) thought that "infinite Good" had derived from the Union, but he understood why the great majority of Scots were opposed to it at the time. In a letter of 4th April 1760 he said of the Union:

> The immediate effect of it was to hurt the interest of every single order of men in the country. The dignity of the nobility was undone by it. The greater part of the Gentry who had been accustomed to represent their own country in its own Parliament were cut out for ever from all hopes of representing it in a British Parliament. Even the merchants seemed to suffer at first. The trade to the Plantations was, indeed, opened to them. But that was a trade which they knew nothing about: the trade they were acquainted with, that to France, Holland and the Baltic, was laid under new embarressments which almost totally annihilated the two first and most important branches of it ... No wonder if at that time all orders of men conspired in cursing a measure so hurtful to their immediate interest.[10]

The vote on the Treaty of some of the landowners in the Scottish Parliament may have been influenced by their concern to maintain the export of cattle to England. Trading interests generally had every reason to be apprehensive. So far from approval of the Treaty resting on hopes of trading advantages, considerations of that kind were not a major factor. Such influence as they had was mainly in the opposite direction. The economic consequences of the Treaty are a distinct question from the motives behind it. They were adverse or neutral for several decades after 1707 and afterwards difficult to distinguish from improvements which were due to other causes. Such economic advantage as might eventually derive from access to a larger market could not be predicted with any confidence when the Treaty was under debate.

Recently Christopher Whateley in his pamphlet, *Bought and sold for English Gold?* has revived the argument that economic considerations were an important factor, or even the major factor, in the vote in the Scottish Parliament. He says that "what mattered ultimately were the votes of the nobility"and that many of them had substantial trading interests. He quotes a phrase in Clerk's *Observations* of 1730 to the effect that trade considerations "had great influence with many."[11] On the first of these points, 42 of the nobility voted for the treaty in the final vote and 19 against; Shires 38 for and 30 against; Burghs 30 for and 20 against. The nobility therefore accounted for only 61 votes out of the total number cast of 179. Many of them were among the recipients of the financial inducements, but only a few were involved in trade mainly those with cattle exports from estates in the Highlands. On the second point, it is very clear from the context of Clerk's remark that he did not suggest that trade was a major consideration. In fact, it is in the same paragraph that he says "the principal motive" was to prevent war and English dominion of Scotland by right of conquest.[12] There is no real evidence to support Whateley's conclusion that a majority of the Scottish Parliament voted for the Union because of "the prospect of obtaining protected trading opportunities."[13]

Whateley also asserts, against all the evidence, that "the incorporating union of 1707 was not a diktat."[14] All contemporary accounts, by members of the administration as well as the opposition, by Mar and Clerk as well as Lockhart, are quite clear that this is precisely what it was. Clerk tell us that the Scottish and English Commissioners met face to face only once. That was about the number of members that Scotland was to be allowed in the joint Parliament, the only point on which the Scots dared to protest.[15]

Again Whateley suggests that members of the Scottish Parliament voted for the Union because they believed that a small country such as Scotland could not "survive and flourish in a threatening world" without the protection of a powerful neighbour.[16] It is true that Seton of Pitmedden, honouring his bargain with the Government, made this point during the debate; but there is no evidence that this opinion was widely shared. Indeed, the Scots had good reasons for believing that the English Government was more intent on destroying Scotland as a commercial rival than in coming to its aid. That was the obvious conclusion to be drawn from long experience of English policy, as in the Navigation Acts and in the pressure against the Darien scheme. As I have mentioned, Fletcher drew attention to the discouraging example of Wales. It is not surprising that the Scottish trading community opposed the Union on commercial, as well as other, grounds.

It is true, as Whatley has pointed out, that there were only nineteen votes in the Scottish Parliament against the clause on the "freedom and intercourse of trade and navigation."[17] This is hardly surprising. Freedom of trade by itself was unobjectionable, and English restrictions on navigation had been a long standing Scottish grievance. Such freedoms were possible even between two independent countries. Votes for this clause cannot be taken to imply that freedom of trade was a motive for supporting the other provisions of the Treaty

It has been argued that the Treaty of Union had a commercial purpose because several of its articles dealt with economic matters. In fact, these articles were concerned with the application of English currency, weights and measures and excise duties to Scotland. They were a necessary consequence of incorporation, not its justification. Whateley has suggested that these articles, and such points as the guarantees to the Scottish Church and to the legal system were concessions won by the Scots, with the implication that the Treaty was to this extent freely negotiated.[18] It does not look like this from the contemporary accounts of the proccedings. The guarantees are much more likely to have been ingenious devices to ease the passage of the Treaty through the Scottish Parliament.

The attempt to give the Union respectability by representing it as a free and rational negotiation in which the Scots sacrficed their independence for reasons of trade is a plausible rationalisation long after the event and it does not stand up to an examination of the contemporary records. On the other hand, Clerk's explanation, even if he played down the part played by bribery, is consistent with the historical evidence. He too was anxious to find a plausible explanation to justify his own part in the transaction. Even so, it was certainly possible that some members of the Scottish Parliament, perhaps a sufficent number to make up a majority, decided that Union was preferable to the risk of invasion and the imposition of worse terms. The one undoubted advantgage of the Union was that it prevented a disastrous war; but the price was abject surrender with all the consequences that flow from that.

References

1   P. W. J. Riley, *The Union of England and Scotland* (Manchester 1978), pp 8,219,281.

2   This correspondence is quoted in the Introduction to *Thoughts on the Union* by A V Dicey and R S Rait. (London 1920), pp2-3.

3   P. Hume Brown, *The Legislative Union of England and Scotland* (Ford Lectures, Oxford 1914), p3.

4   In George Baillie of Jerviswoode, *Correspondence, 1702-1708* (Bannatyne Club, Vol. 72, 1842), pp138,97,28.

5   Paul H Scott, *Andrew Fletcher and the Treaty of Union,* (Edinburgh 1992 and 1994), pp85-7.

6   Andrew Fletcher of Saltoun, Speech to the Scottish Parliament, 1703, in *Selected Political Writings and Speeches of Andrew Fletcher of Saltoun,* ed. David Daiches (Edinburgh 1979), pp119-120.

7   George Lockhart of Carnwath, *'Scotland's Ruine': Lockhart of Carnwath's Memoirs of the Union* (Aberdeen 1995), p.152.

8   Daniel Defoe, *A Tour Thro' the Whole Island of Great Britain* (London 1727), Vol. III, p33.

9   Sir John Clerk of Penicuik, *Observations* (1730), in Scottish History Society, *Miscellany X,* (Edinburgh 1965), pp182,212.

10   Adam Smith, *Correspondence*, ed. E C Mossner and I S Ross, (Glasgow 1994), p68.

11   Christopher Whateley, *Bought and Sold for English Gold* (Glasgow 1994), p31.

12   Sir John Clerk, *op. cit.*, p191.
13   Christopher Whateley, *op. cit.*, p47.
14   *Ibid.* p47.
15   Sir John Clerk of Penicuik, *History of the Union of Scotland and England*, translated and edited by Douglas Duncan, (Edinburgh SHS 1993), p85.
16   Whateley, *op. cit.*, p33.
17   *Ibid.* p36.
18   *Ibid.* pp37-38.

CHAPTER 4

The Century of Neglect

After their determined effort to secure the Union, the English Government were content with their success and for most of the rest of the century took very little further interest in Scotland. They made no attempt to treat Scotland as they had treated Ireland with the deliberate intrusion of an alien ruling class. It might be said that this was unnecessary when they could count on the co-operation of the class of Scots who had accepted English appointment, payment and instruction in the Scottish Parliament. Corruption had helped to achieve the Union; it now became the mechanism by which it was continued. A pamphlet of the time (which may have been at least partly written by Andrew Fletcher) said that it was easier to corrupt the 45 Scottish members in the British Parliament in London than the 300 in the Scottish Parliament in Edinburgh.[1] English restraint in exploiting their advantage is to their credit, but it was also sensible politically. The majority in the Scottish Parliament had not been achieved easily and the Scottish people as a whole were clearly hostile to the Union. There was no point in putting it at risk by any further provocation.

Tom Devine, in an admirable analysis of the effects of the Union, has suggested that a possible explanation of this restraint is that the English Government "wanted parliamentary union with the Scots for reasons of military and political security and had no economic ambitions north of the Border."[2] There is no doubt that security considerations were predominant, but English Governments had always been anxious to prevent Scotland becoming a serious competitor in trade. In his *Observations* of 1730 Sir John Clerk said that there was "a moral certainty that England would never allow us to grou rich and pouerfull in a separat state."[3] This was the thought behind the English Navigation Acts which confined trade with their colonies to English ships and English merchants. The removal of the Lord Advocate's clause when the Scottish Act of Security was given royal assent in 1704 was in line with this attitude. So were the measures to frustrate the Scottish Company of the Darien scheme and its abolition by the Treaty of Union. After the Treaty came into force, the British Parliament only a tew years later ignored it in legislation which was to the disadvantage of Scottish trade by imposing a duty on the export of linen in 1711 and a duty on malt in 1713. Apart from some transgressions such as these, the Treaty in fact created a customs union and a common market. English trading interests had evidently been persuaded to drop their traditional objections to them because of the advantages of abolishing the potential military and political threat of an independent Scotland. Also Scotland, where manufactures were less highly developed that in England, offered a useful market for English goods.

The conspicuous exception to the post-union restraint was, of course, in the ruthless reaction to the Jacobite rising of 1745. This was a threat, not only to the Hanoverian royal line, but also once again to the English control of Scotland because the repeal of the Union was one of the objectives of the rising. Individual Scots were presented with a difficult choice. Jacobitism offered an escape from the Union and a return to traditional Scottish values, of "old Scottish faith, hospitality, worth and honour", as Sir Walter Scott said in the Postscript to *Waverley*. On the other hand, Jacobitism was also associated with Catholicism or Episcopalianism, both of which were rejected by most Scots at that time, and with arbitrary royal power. This produced such an acute dilemma that it invited indecision, followed by guilt and embarrassment.

After Culloden, Cumberland's forces suppressed the Highlands with a barbarity which amounted to genocide and which nearly destroyed the Highland way of life. It was accompanied by legislation of the British Parliament with the same purpose, the Disarming Act, the banning of Highland dress and the abolition of the heritable jurisdictions. This last was in violation of the Treaty of Union which had guaranteed these jurisdictions, that is the right of landowners to act as judges on their own estates. The effect of these measures was to convert chiefs with a responsibility for their clans into landowners concerned with their rents. The Highland clearances, which depopulated the Highlands by driving people from the land, were a direct consequence.

Outside the Highlands the ruthlessness of the Hanoverian reaction had different, but profound effects. It marked the the extinction of any hope of escape from the Union in the foreseeable future and therefore encouraged a resigned acceptance of it. Probably also it created a general nervousness. Opposition to the Union had become a symptom of Jacobitism and that was treasonable. The horror of what had happened to the Highlands was a warning of what might happen to people who indulged in such dangerous thoughts.

The consequences of this tension and nervousness are visible in the books of the literary men of the Scottish Enlightenment who were writing their major works in the years which followed Culloden. They were enlarging the horizons of thought by the free exercise of the mind on nearly every conceivable subject, except Scotland itself. They wrote extensively about the nature of human society and its historical evolution. The Scotland which surrounded them was going through a process of rapid and drastic change; but nearly always they avoided any discussion of the Scottish situation and drew their examples from almost anywhere else, usually from ancient Greece and Rome or contemporary north America. Their inhibitions are obvious. Quite apart from the risk of a charge of Jacobitism, they also had to avoid giving offence to the aristocratic patrons on whom they depended for their academic appointments, highly desirable jobs as escorts on a grand tour or even, since the British Parliament had imposed patronage on the Scottish Church in 1712, presentation as a minister of the Kirk. "While it may be argued", Richard Finlay wrote in a recent essay, "that the intellectual frenzy of Enlightenment

Scotland was a patriotic response to the loss of nationhood and parliament, it must never be forgotten that the climate in which the intelligentsia operated was determined by the need to defend the political *status quo* and the aristocratic patronage upon which most intellectuals depended for their livelihood."[4] This system of patronage was closely linked to the "managed", or corrupted, representation in the British Parliament.

But the literati of the Enlightenment did, occasionally and discreetly   reveal that they regretted the loss of independence and saw advantage in cultural diversity and the independence of small nations. In his letters, but not in his published works, David Hume made no secret of his feelings about England in such remarks as: "the Barbarians who inhabit the Banks of the Thames"; "the daily and hourly Progress of Madness and Folly and Wickedness in England"; and "it has been my misfortune to write in the language of the most stupid and factious Barbarians in the world."[5]   In his essay, *Of the Rise of the Arts and Sciences*, he followed very closely Andrew Fletcher's argument in his *Account of a Conversation* about the advantages of diversity as in the city states of ancient Greece. In another essay, *Idea of a Perfect Commonwealth*, he said that "a small commonwealth is the happiest government in the world within itself, because everything lies under the eye of the rulers". He conceded that "it may be subdued by great force from without."[6] Perhaps this was a reference to the Union.

Adam Ferguson in his very influential book, *Essay on the History of a Civil Society* (1767), said that it was not necessary to enlarge communities in order to enjoy the advantages of living in society: "We frequently obtain them in the most remarkable degree, where nations remain independent, and are of a small extent."[7] Another of the major writers of the Scottish Enlightenment, John Millar, said in *The Origins of the Distinction of Ranks* (1771) that the people of small states "have been commonly sucessful in their efforts to establish a free constitution", but that "extensive nations were much more likely to end in tyranny." [8] I mentioned in the last chapter a letter of Adam Smith of April 1760 in which he said that the Union had brought advantages, but elsewhere he too expessed views in favour of the independence of small states and against centralised control. In *The Wealth of Nations* (1776) he said that the colonies of ancient Greece had flourished because "they had plenty of good land, and as they were altogether independent of the mother city were at liberty to manage their own affairs in the way that they judged was most suitable to their own interest". The Roman colonies, on the other hand, were "by no means so brilliant" precisely because they were not independent. Smith went on to consider modern colonies and came to the conclusion that the conditions of prosperity for all of them were the availability of good land and the independence to manage their own affairs.[9]

Why then did Smith in 1760 think that the Union had brought "infinite Good" and the people as a whole were no longer opposed to it? At the time he was not alone in thinking this. Only a few years later, on 26th December 1765, James Boswell recorded a conversation in Avignon with an exiled Jacobite, Lord Dunbar, who asked him if most people in Scotland were now reconciled to the Union. Boswell, who throughout his life bitterly regretted the Union, replied: "My lord, I fear they are; that is to say, they have lost all principle and spirit of patriotism."[10]

We might expect to find some explanation of Smith's view of the Union in his published works. In the *Wealth of Nations* he makes two points about the economic effects. The Union, he remarks, brought an increase in the price of cattle because of the demand from England and continues: "Of all the commercial advantages, however, which Scotland has derived from the union with England (without saying what these were) this rise in the price of cattle is, perhaps, the greatest. It has not only raised the value of all highland estates, but it has, perhaps, been the principal cause of the improvement of the low country". On the other hand: "The wool of

Scotland fell very considerably in its price in consequence of the union with England, by which it was excluded from the great market of Europe, and confined to the narrow one of Great Britain."[11]

This balance of economic advantage and disadvantage does not sound like a strong endorsement of the Union on economic grounds alone. Scottish historians of the present generally take an equally equivocal view. Michael Lynch in his *Scotland: A New History* says that discussion of the long -term economic effect of the Union is "a largely artificial exercise which is ultimately subjective rather than scientific."[12] We know what happened after the Union; we do not know what would have happened without it and cannot therefore make a rational comparison. Tom Devine says that the Union "offered risks as well as opportunities in almost equal measure. Integration could have meant Scotland's reduction to the status of an English economic satellite, a supplier of foods, raw materials and labour for the English economy, but with little possibility of pronounced economic diversification in her own right...... Ultimately what mattered, therefore, was the Scottish reaction in the new context and the influences which conditioned this response."[13]

Devine also thinks that Smith exaggerated the importance of the cattle trade. It did increase after the Union and made money for some landlords in the Highlands and Galloway, but "neither of these areas were in the van of agrarian progress" and because cattle were exported on the hoof, the trade had little effect on the infra-structure. It is surprising that Smith does not mention the tobacco trade, the foundation of the wealth of Glasgow. This had begun before the Union, but Scottish trade with the English colonies was then against English law, which was a handicap. The trade expanded after the Union; but, as Devine says, "the Union did not cause the growth of the tobacco trade. That came about because Scots merchants adopted more efficient commercial practices than their rivals." This was evident after the American declaration of independence in 1783 when Scottish and other British merchants no longer had special privileges in the market. The Scots quickly re-established the American link and established new trades to the Caribbean, Europe and eventually to Latin America and the East Indies. The Scottish industrial economy began to expand significantly precisely at this time which is a strong indication that the Union was not a major factor.[14]

Scotland had a number of inherent advantages which contributed to the economic expansion towards the end of the 18th century. In the first place, the social and intellectual climate was favourable to economic improvement in both agriculture and industry. The first essay about new farming methods was published as early as 1595 and some of the new methods began to be adopted at the start of the 17th century.[15] Andrew Fletcher was one of those who advocated improvements in the 1690s. The 18th century in Scotland was a period when there were no rigid barriers between intellectual disciplines and saw no reason why the same mind should not address questions of farming or industrial chemistry as well as those of philosophy. Lord Kames, for instance, wrote about morality, natural religion, law and literary criticism, but also about the application of rational principles to the improvement of agriculture. James Watt's workshop was "a kind of academy whether all the notabilities of Glasgow repaired, to discuss the nicest questions in art, science, and literature."[6] It was in this workshop, of course, that Watt made the improvements to the steam engine which transformed the industry and transport of the world. The most influential social class of the time, the lairds, had relations of family or friendship with the intellectuals and academics and ideas circulated easily between them. They shared a common interest in improvement. There was an intelligent and educated population, as well as the advantages of deep water estuaries and close proximity of deposits of coal and iron ore.

The conclusion of the economic historian, R. H. Campbell, is that "the impact of the Union neither produced a new economic problem nor a ready -made solution ... There was a chronological, if not a logical, connection between the Union and economic growth, and that was as far as most people took their analysis ... The Union assisted but did not cause economic growth; economic growth made the Union acceptable."[17] In other words, one of the reasons why the Union was generally accepted after about 1760 was increasing prosperity. This was mainly due to efforts by the Scots themselves, but since it followed the Union, there was a tendency to give it the credit. As R. J. Finlay said in a recent book: "When the Scottish economy began to flourish, the key factors in expansion are due to Scottish initiative and enterprise. In short, the Scottish economy boomed because the Scots made it boom."[18]

Adam Smith makes a curious remark in the *Wealth of Nations* about the political consequences of the Union: "By the Union with England the middling and inferior ranks of people in Scotland gained a complete deliverance from the power of an aristocracy which had always before oppressed them."[19] There was, in fact, more rather than less aristocratic control of Scotland from the Union until at least the Reform Act of 1832. Such government as there was from London was in the hands of a succession of aristocratic managers, such as the Earl of Islay (afterwards 3rd Duke of Argyll) who acted as "the uncrowned ruler of Scotland" from 1725 to 1761.[20] Perhaps Smith was thinking of the abolition of the heritable jurisdictions after the '45, but they had not been abolished, but guaranteed by the Treaty of Union. Their abolition was desirable, but they had long before ceased to be a serious means of oppression.

With the exception of the suppression of the Highlands after the '45, the Union made remarkably little difference to the lives of the Scottish people throughout the 18th century. "The truth of the matter is that life went on much the same as it had always done. The people who governed Scotland were the same, the legal system was the same and the Church maintained its pervasive role in Scottish society."[21] When James Stuart Mackenzie, the brother of the Earl of Bute, took over in 1761 as minister responsible for Scottish affairs he could find no papers in his office to suggest that any business was being carried on.[22] "Between 1727 and 1745 only nine Acts of Parliament dealt specifically with Scotland, seven of them of little consequence.[23] The Government were concerned only by the exercise of patronage to prevent the Scottish Members of Parliament making any trouble.

After the alarms of 1745, Westminster returned to the same lethargic indifference. In his *Letters of Malachi Malagrowther* of 1826, Sir Walter Scott described the situation:

> Scotland, no longer the object of terror, or at least great uneasiness, to the British Government, was left from the year 1750 under the guardianship of her own institutions to win her silent way to national wealth and consequence ... But neglected as she was, and perhaps because she was neglected, Scotland, reckoning her progress during the space from the close of the American war to the present day has increased her prosperity in a ratio more than five times greater than that of her more fortunate and richer sister.[24]

This sister, by which he means England, had not actively assisted in this progress, but at least had not intervened to hamper it.

There were therefore several reasons why the Union became generally accepted in Scotland from about 1760. It had meant less interference than had been feared; the country was becoming more prosperous; people had become accustomed to the new situation and there was in any case no practical hope of escape.

References

1   Attributed to Andrew Fletcher of Saltoun, *State of the Controversy Betwixt United and Separate Parliaments* (1706), ed. P H Scott, (Edinburgh 1982), p23.

2   T M Devine, *Exploring the Scottish Past* (East Linton 1995), p44.

3   Sir John Clerk of Penicuik, *Observations* (1730), in Scottish History Society, *Miscellany X*, (Edinburgh 1965), p192.

4   Richard Finlay, 'Caledonia or North Britain' in *Image and Identity*, ed. D Broun, R J Finlay and M Lynch, (Edinburgh 1998), p.146.

5   David Hume, *Letters*, ed. J Y T Greig, (Oxford 1932), Vol. I, p436, Vol II, pp208,209.

6   David Hume, *Selected Essays*, ed. Stephen Copley and Andrew Edger, (Oxford 1993), pp64,311.

7   Adam Ferguson, *Essay on the History of Civil Society* (1767), ed. Duncan Forbes (Edinburgh 1966), p59.

8   John Millar, *The Origins of the Distinction of Ranks* (1771), extract in *The Scottish Enlightenment:An Anthology*, ed. Alexander Broadie (Edinburgh 1997), p542.

9   Adam Smith, *The Wealth of Nations* (1776), Everman's Library edition (London 1971), Vol. II, (Book IV, Chapter VII), pp64-5,69.

10   James Boswell, *Boswell on the Grand Tour: Italy, Corsica and France*, ed. F Brady and F A Pottle, (London 1955), p266.

11   Adam Smith, *op. cit.*, Vol I, (Book I, Chapter XI), pp204,216.

12   Michael Lynch, *Scotland: A New History,* (London 1991), p323.

13   T M Devine, *op. cit.*, p42.

14   *Ibid.* pp.45,45-46.

15   Alexander Fenton, 'Scottish Agriculture and the Union: An Example
16   of Indigenous Development' in *The Union of 1707: Its Impact on Scotland*, ed. by T I Rae (Glasgow 1974), p79.
      Neil McCallum, *A Small Country* (Edinburgh 1983), p99.

17   R H Campbell, 'The Union and Economic Growth' in *The Union of 1707: Its Impact on Scotland*, *op. cit.*, pp72-3.

18   Richard Finlay, *op. cit.*, p145.

19   Adam Smith, *op. cit.*, Vol.II, (Book V, Chapter III), p427.

20   Michael Lynch, *op. cit.*, p324.

21   Alexander Murdoch, *'The People Above': Politics and Administration in Mid Eighteenth Century Scotland* (Edinburgh 1980), p106.

22   T M Devine, *op. cit.*, p44.

23   Sir Walter Scott, *The Letters of Malachi Malagrowther* (1826), ed. P H Scott, (Edinburgh 1981), p10.

CHAPTER 5

The Age of Empire

The purpose of Sir Walter Scott's *Letters of Malachi Malagrowther*, however, was not to celebrate Scotland's freedom from Westminster interference in the 18th century, but to protest against it in the century which followed. In 1826 the British Government, not for the first or the last time applying to Scotland a solution for an English problem, proposed to prohibit the issue of one pound notes by the banks. In Scotland, although not in England at that time, the banks were sound and reliable. The Scottish economy was largely run on their one pound notes and their suppression would have been a serious disruption. For Scott this was the last straw, the latest in a series of measures to change everything in Scotland to an English model" whether it was to the benefit of Scotland or not. He thought that this was both insulting and dangerous and it had been disturbing him for years. "I am certainly serious in Malachi if seriousness will do good", he wrote to his partner and publisher, James Ballantyne, "I will sleep quieter in my grave for having so fair an opportunity of speaking my mind."[1]

The *Malachi* letters were concerned with a disturbing change in the English attitude to Scotland:

A spirit of proselytism has of late shown itself in England for extending the benefits of their system, in all its strength and weakness, to a country, which has been hitherto flourishing and contented under its own. They adopted the conclusion, that all English enactments are right; but the system of municipal law in Scotland is not English, therefore it is wrong.[2]

This attitude, which has been the source of Scottish complaints from that day to this, began to be shown, Scott says, in "the last fifteen or twenty years, and more especially in the last ten."[3] In other words, it had become particularly apparent from about 1815, the year of the Battle of Waterloo. It was from that time, and for the next century or so, that Britain became the dominant power in the world. London, self-confident in its wealth and prestige, saw little reason to concern itself with the distinctiveness or the feelings of the Scots.

It was also at this time that the emerging idea of Great Britain as an entity was strengthened by the shared experience of the Napoleonic Wars. Linda Colley in her influential book, *Britons: Forging the Nation, 1707-1837* described Britain as "an invented nation superimposed, if only for a while, onto much older alignments and loyalties.... It was an invention forged above all by war", and the war was against France. The British "defined themselves as Protestants struggling for survival against the world's foremost Catholic power,"[4] There were wars which might be so described during the 18th century; but, as R. J. Finlay has pointed out, when the most significant of them was fought, it was no longer against a Catholic country but against a post-revolutionary state which had renounced religion.[5]

This raises the question of the extent to which this anti-French, anti-Catholic British ideology embraced the majority of Scots. The Protestant churches of Scotland and England were very different and Scottish Presbyterians in the 18th and 19th centuries were unlikely to feel a sense of close identity with English Episcopalians. At the time of the French Revolution, the ruling establishment were certainly terrified of the possibility of the spread of revolutionary ideas from France. Many other people, perhaps a majority, were more likely to welcome them, like Thomas Muir or Robert Burns. Towards the end of his life Burns was threatened with an official investigation into his political views; he might have been tried and deported like Muir and his friends. In self defence he joined the Dumfries Volunteers and wrote an anti-French song for them. But, as he said in a letter to Mrs Dunlop on 6th December 1792: "What my private sentiments are, you will find out without an Interpreter."

I think that Richard Finlay was right to ask, "was this British identity a national identity or was it an élite identity confined to the upper reaches of society?" [6] Tom Nairn has offered an answer: "'Britain' was a multi-national social class before it was a multi-national state; and the latter remains in essence a manifestation of the former."[7] Linda Colley describes this multi-national class:

> Rich, landed and talented nobs from Wales, Scotland, England and to a lesser extent Ireland became welded after the 1770s into a single ruling class that intermarried, shared the same outlook, and took to itself the business of governing, fighting for, and profiting from, greater Britain.[8]

In so far as wars forged a sense of British identity, those of the 20th century against Germany were much more potent than the earlier wars against France. The German wars involved the whole population because of conscription and air attacks and because propaganda had become much more sophisticated and wide-spread.

Meanwhile, in the course of the 19th century, the Empire became the major manifestation of Britishness. Michael Lynch in his *Scotland: A New History* says that the Scots embraced, not Britain, but "a British Empire which opened up in the 1780s and disappeared after 1945."[9] The Empire offered jobs and trading opportunities to far more people than the ruling class alone and therefore created, in Scotland more than in England, a certain idea of Britain. Colley has a good description of this process:

> For some Scots, though, it was less the job and trading opportunities that empire provided, than the idea of empire that proved most compelling. If Britain's primary identity was to be an imperial one, then the English were put firmly and for ever in their place, reduced to a component part of a much greater whole, exactly like the Scots, and no longer the people who ran the whole show. A British imperium, in other words, enabled Scots to feel themselves peers of the English in a way still denied them in an island kingdom. The language bears this out very clearly. The English and the foreign are still all too inclined today to refer to the island of Great Britain as 'England'. But at no time have they ever customarily referred to an English empire. When it existed, as in retrospect, the empire has always been emphatically British. In terms of

self-respect, then, as well as the profits it could bestow, imperialism served as Scotland's opportunity. [10]

This is not the whole story. To Scots in the 19th century, the Empire was not only an opportunity for trade and jobs and a substitute for satisfaction in what was happening in Scotland itself, it was also a source of pride in the discharge of a moral responsibility. Strange as it may now seem, the Empire was regarded, in the words of Graham Walker, "as a force for moral and social progress" in a vast area of the world, and the impulse behind this was Scottish Presbyterianism.[11] A Scottish doctor in the Indian Army wrote home to his children at school in Edinburgh about the St. Andrew's day dinner in Bombay in 1910. There were pipers, he said, and very good speeches, "all about Scotland and the great men who had gone out of it to help to rule great lands and to do good in all parts of the world. It is surely a great privilege to belong to such a land and we must try to be good and great men for Auld Scotland's sake". The writer who quotes this, Elizabeth Hay, comments that "Scots participated in the Empire as Scots. They did not in any way feel it was England's Empire." [12]

The idea of Britishness associated with the Empire was not an all-embracing national identity which displaced and replaced the long established national identities. In Scotland this Britishness was seen as something separate from, and compatible with, the continued existence of Scotland as a nation with its own sense of national identity. Britishness meant participation as a partner in a great imperial undertaking and that was some compensation for the loss of independence. The English saw little need to agonise about these questions; in any case they have never clearly distinguished between England and Britain. To the extent that they thought about it at all, they were perfectly content to leave the Scots with their own view of these matters. It was in their interest to do so because the Empire could hardly have been administered or defended without the Scottish contribution.

Also, as a recent book has pointed out, the English have not been particularly interested in the active cultural assimilation of Scotland: "Loyalty to the Crown, obedience to Parliament, tolerance of Church establishment, and acceptance of English as the primary public language constituted the principal pillars of the Unionist state. Crucially there was no formal attempt to make Britishness a primary cultural identity".[13] There is clearly an element of truth in this in the sense that British Governments have never had a conscious and comprehensive policy of cultural imposition. At the same time, the acceptance of the English language, like Latin in the Roman Empire, was a very profound cultural change. The parallel with Latin is very close. As Tacitus said of the ancient Britons, "Instead of loathing the Latin language they became eager to speak it effectively.. ..They thought that it was a mark of civilisation, when in fact it was a feature of their enslavement."[14] Much the same could be said of the anxiety of some circles in Edinburgh in the 1760s to learn English, a fashion which subsequently spread to other parts of the country and eventually to the schools, strongly abetted in this century by radio and television. If Gaelic and Scots did not have an inherent resilience, they would have been eradicated long since.

Of course, English is now a major means of international communication, largely, as David Hume predicted,[15] because of the power of the United States. The fact that is also now the "primary public language" in Scotland has obvious advantages. That does not mean that the efforts to suppress Gaelic and Scots have not had their price. Both languages have impressive literatures which are an essential part of our cultural identity. Like all languages, they embody centuries of shared experience and therefore express, as imported or imposed languages cannot, aspects of the character which has emerged from that experience. The loss of any language is an impoverishment of human diversity. Also we have to consider the effect on children of an educational system which dismisses as unacceptable their first language, the language of their parents. This can easily destroy their self-confidence and ability to communicate.

It can lead to a sense of inadequacy and even self-hate. Michael Hechter and others have argued that colonising powers denigrate the culture of dependent territories in order to undermine their will to resist and that this achieved "through the voluntary assimilation of peripheral élites."[16] The attack on Gaelic and Scots by our schools has been such a policy of denigration and those responsible, consciously or not, have been such an assimilated élite.

The humiliations of the way in which the Union was achieved and of the treatment of the Highlands after the '45, the loss of independence, of the self-respect of responsibility and of an international identity, all of these, as well as the contempt of the élite for our own languages and culture, were likely to inflict psychological damage. C. J. Watson has suggested that the novels of Neil Gunn reveal the effects of such things on the Highlands in particular: "the sense of weariness, of the absence of hope, and of lacerating self-contempt which is a marked component in the psyche of 'colonised' peoples". [17] Trevor Royle has remarked that "no country under the domination of another can ever shake off its sense of inferiority."[18] Many observers have detected these qualities among some people in present day Scotland.[19] Fortunately, there has been a recovery of confidence and there is now a strong movement away from the policy of denigration. It is late in the day, but not, I think, too late. The old policy of the schools was mistaken, but it was carried out with what they thought to be good intentions. Partly it was because of a desire to equip the pupils for employment in England and the Empire. The schools have been described as factories for the manufacture of emigrants,[20] part of the cost of the Union and the Empire.

The attempt of the British Government "to change everything to an English model", about which Sir Walter Scott protested with such vigour, did not go very far in the course of the 19th century. Partly this was because the role of Government and Parliament in affecting everyday life was still very limited. The law, the Church, the local authorities, the schools and universities - all still distinctively Scottish - had much more impact. This was autonomy of a kind. In fact, Lindsay Paterson in his book, *The Autonomy of Modern Scotland*, has demonstrated that Scotland, at any rate until quite recent times, has been more autonomous than many other European countries that were nominally independent.[21] But it was a highly unsatisfactory form of autonomy. There was no central authority to hold the country together nor even any body, except to some extent the General Assembly of the Church of Scotland which met for only one week each year, to debate and consider the over-all situation of the country. There was, as R. H. Campbell has said, "no really effective Scottish administration from the Union until the institution of the Scottish Office in 1885."[22] Whenever there was a need for new legislation, or the amendment of laws to meet changing conditions, it was very difficult to persuade the Government of the day to take an interest, or to find parliamentary time, for a purely Scottish issue.

An outstanding example of this difficulty was over the question of lay patronage in the appointment of ministers in the Church of Scotland. This was the consequence of an Act passed by the British Parliament in 1712, in violation of the guarantees given at the time of the Union, to impose the English system of the choice of ministers by the landowners, a direct challenge to the conviction of the Church of Scotland that the congregations had the right to choose their ministers. The conflict which this created between lairds and congregations became a serious crisis by the early decades of the 19th century. In spite of all the Church could do by rational argument and persuasion, the Governmen refused to take any action to deal with the problem which their predecessors had caused. Lord Cockburn, one of the shrewdest and best informed observers of the time, commented:

There never was such an instance of the habitual ignorance and indifference of Government (all governments) to Scotch affairs as in this of patronage: - a deep, vital and pressing question - kindred to others in the English and Irish churches, and in which one plain course was clearly pointed out by responsible and consulted Scotch advisers; yet because it was <u>as yet</u> merely Scotch, and conducted without turbulent agitation, it was impossible to get <u>any line whatever</u> adopted by ministers. This has long been the established system for managing this part of the empire. [23]

The consequence was the Disruption of 1843 when 430 ministers, about a third of the total, walked out of the General Assembly to establish a separate Free Church, abandoning their kirks, manses and incomes. This was heroic. "It is one of the rarest occurrences in moral history", wrote Lord Cockburn in his *Journal*, "I know of no parallel to it."[24] It was followed by the equally heroic effort to build new kirks, manses, halls and schools all over Scotland from the contributions of the congregations. It was a magnificent effort, eloquent of the public spirit and commitment to moral principle of the Scottish people; but it was also a major distraction. Since the loss of the Parliament, the Church of Scotland had been the sole remaining unifying force in Scottish life and the main provider of education and social services. Now the Church was preoccupied for the rest of the century with this internal problem at a time of increasing social tension because of the growth of industry and the movement of people from the country to the towns. It was the worst disaster in internal Scottish affairs since the Clearances and, like the Clearances, it was a direct consequence of the Union.

From 1843 onwards, therefore, Scotland was even more headless and defenceless against the pressures of the time. The Empire provided careers for individual Scots as administrators, teachers, missionaries, soldiers, doctors and engineers. Scottish industry, still under Scottish ownership and control, served the needs of the Empire for ships and locomotives. The Scottish talent and energy that went into the development of the Empire was denied to Scotland itself because there was no Parliament or Goverment committed to the needs of the country as a whole, as distinct from authorities for particular areas or functions. "People degenerate", Eric Linklater said, "when they lose control of their own affairs", and Edwin Muir: Scotland was falling to pieces, for there was "no visible and effective power to hold it together."[25] One symptom of this was emigration on a massive scale which still continued when Muir wrote in 1935: "Scotland is gradually being emptied of its population, its spirit, its wealth, industry art, intellect, and innate character ... If a country exports its most enterprising spirits and best minds year after year, for fifty or a hundred or two hundred years, some result will inevitably follow."[26]

In his volume of the *Edinburgh History of Scotland, 1689 to the Present*, William Ferguson says that after 1827 (in other words, at about the time of Scott's *Malachi* letters) "Scotland came to be treated as a province rather than a partner ... Gradually, there arose a feeling that Scotland was ill-used", particularly over Government expenditure.[27] Lord Rosebery said that Scotland was the "milch cow" of the Empire and was not getting her just deserts.[28] A province can be well governed, but Scotland was not so much governed as exploited. It was a convenient source of talented administrators to run the Empire and of soldiers to risk, and lose, their lives in its defence; but there was very little sign of any serious concern on the part of the Government to attend to the well-being of the country. Because of the availability of coal and iron ore, and of Scottish enterprise, Scotland became, as Christopher Harvie says, "by any standards a substantial world industrial power";[29] but the housing of the workers and their standards of health were allowed to fall to scandalously low levels, from which they have not yet recovered.

In a passage which I quoted from Gordon Donaldson in the Introduction, he gave 1853 as the year in which there began "a series of waves of unrest in which the Union has been attacked and challenged" and which have continued ever since. He chose 1853 because that was when the Association for the Vindication of Scottish Rights, the first organisation of its kind, was formed. "It was warmly backed by most of the town councils in Scotland, by several commissioners of supply, and by many professional bodies. The outcome of numerous well-attended public meetings was over fifty petitions to the government."[30] Like Sir Walter Scott, they did not go so far as to demand the repeal of the Union, which was not then within the scope of political possibility; but they insisted on respect for the guarantees contained in the Treaty.

It was these guarantees which had preserved a degree of autonomy for Scotland, and its distinctive character, as long as the Church, the law and the system of education were free from interference and had more influence on the lives of the people than a distant and inactive Parliament. Because of this, Lindsay Paterson is able to say, somewhat paradoxically, that "the dominant theme of nineteenth-century Scottish politics is successful nationalism."[31] The English authority on constitutional questions, A. V. Dicey, and the Scottish historian, R. S. Rait, published a long and elaborate joint book in defence of the Union in 1920. One of their conclusions was that "the supreme glory of the Act" (they mean, of course, the Acts of the two Parliaments which ratified the Treaty) was "that while creating the political unity it kept alive the nationalism both of England and of Scotland."[32]

The treaty unfortunately left Scotland at the mercy of the whim of the House of Commons. It contained no provision for the arbitration of disputes and nothing to prevent Parliament, following the English doctrine of parliamentary sovereignty, legislating as it pleased whether it was in conformity with the Treaty or not. One of the reasons for the increasing discontent with the Union was because such interference, although still comparatively restrained by modern standards, was becoming more frequent. The elementary school system was fragmented as a consequence of the Disruption, "making it difficult to maintain a distinctive Scottish educational tradition; this opened the door to the Anglicizers."[33] The Scottish universities, which had been much more successful than the English in the 18th century, were gradually forced to comply with the English model.

This process is the subject of George Davie's great book, *The Democratic Intellect*, in which he describes "the tortuous, dark revolution whereby a nation noted educationally both for social mobility and for fixity of first principle gradually reconciled itself to an alien system in which principles traditionally did not matter and a rigid social immobilism was the accepted thing."[34] For such reasons as these, the guarantees of the Treaty were beginning to look threadbare by about the middle of the 19th century.

The obvious question therefore is why has it taken nearly 150 years of discontent, discussion and agitation for any substantial change to be achieved in the constitutional arrangements of 1707. In the first place, there was what Allan Massie has called the "nineteenth-century commitment to the imperial idea ... separatism in the Victorian noonday was a crank's game."[35] The sheer prestige and power of the British state, at the time when it was the strongest and richest country in the world, was a formidable challenge. It not only had the levers of power in its hands, but also most of the means of propaganda, including the monarchy. The success of this propaganda machine is evident in the number of completely false myths about the Union and the British constitution which it has persuaded most people to accept as unquestionable truths. Another important factor was quite simply the political impotence of the mass of the population until the right to vote was gradually extended to them in the course of the 19th and early 20th centuries.

One of the historical myths which has been firmly fixed in the minds of the people is that of the perfection of the constitution derived from the "Glorious Revolution" of 1688-9. In the letter which Robert Burns felt obliged to write, to avoid investigation and possible prosecution in January 1793, he said: "I look upon the British Constitution, as settled at the Revolution, to be the most glorious constitution on earth, or that perhaps the wit of man can frame."[36] He did not believe it, of course, but that was more or less the accepted formula. The 1688 settlement in England and 1689 in Scotland did give more freedom of debate to the Parliaments of both countries, and therefore to the British Parliament which followed; but these Parliaments, then and for long after, represented only a small part of the population. In Scotland the population at that time was about 2.3 million, but until the Reform Act of 1832 only 3,000 people had the right to vote. The successive Reform Acts which followed widened the franchise, but it was a slow process. By 1886, 28.5% of British men over 21 had the vote, but it was only fully extended to women in 1922. From about the middle of the 19th century many other European countries had more generous franchises than the British. Linda Colley concludes that "the United Kingdom remained, right up to the First World War, one of the least democratic states by the standards of eastern as well as western Europe."[37] For most of the 19th century only men of some property had the vote. For the most part, they were Tom Nairn's "multi-national social class" who were doing well out of the constitutional *status quo* and therefore disinclined to risk change.

The Union meant, of course, that in Britain only the British parliament could legislate for electoral reform or for reform of any kind. It followed that Scottish politicians who wanted reform had to work with like-minded people in England. Since the population of England was so much larger they had to accept the English agenda and work at the English pace and in accord with the English historical myths. Only the English precedents counted and the Scottish egalitarian traditions and democratic aspirations had no relevance in this respect. Colin Kidd has suggested that this made Scotland "in a sense a 'historyless' nation."[38] Parliamentary reform in Scotland became, in the words of Michael Dyer, "the process by which procedures inherited from an independent Scotland were gradually rejected in favour of a uniform system encompassing the whole of the United Kingdom."[39] Reform was therefore almost invariably also anglicisation and was criticised by the Tories on precisely these grounds. The Conservative historian, Michael Fry, refers to "the usual ruthless anglicisation of the Whigs."[40] The Whig historians have created a myth that there was some particular virtue, and a monopoly of wisdom, in the English parliamentary tradition and that it was only because of this that reform was possible. It would follow from this that Scotland could only benefit from it by means of the Union. In fact, as we have seen, there was a very slow and reluctant march by the British Parliament of more than two centuries towards anything resembling democracy. There are several reasons for the alternative opinion that Scotland would have evolved a satisfactory democracy much more quickly if we had remained independent. The Scottish doctrine that sovereignty rests with the people is the foundation of a democratic approach. It was implied in the Declaration of Arbroath of 1320 and given substantial intellectual substance by George Buchanan in the 16th century.[41] There is plenty of evidence in Scottish literature that a spirit of egalitarianism and of concern for others has prevailed in Scotland for many centuries. From Buchanan onwards Scotland produced a succession of brilliant political thinkers, such as Fletcher, Hume, Ferguson and Millar, all concerned with progress towards a fair and free society. The debates in the Scottish Parliament in 1703 and 1704, and the general acceptance of the proposals of Andrew Fletcher, showed that enlightened ideas were already widely supported. Fletcher had in effect proposed the transfer of all the powers of the royal prerogative from the monarch to parliament. This is something which the British Parliament has not yet achieved.

Then there is the record of legislation by the Scottish Parliament.The Scottish Parliament has had a bad press in the hands of the Whig historians, a reflection of the attitude that if it is not English it must be wrong. A comparison of the legislation of the two Parliaments suggests a different conclusion, as James MacKinnon suggested in his book, *The Union of England and Scotland* first published in 1896:

> It has been contended not without reason that the old Scottish Parliament had anticipated many of those reforms, which it has been the endeavour

of modern liberalism to secure for the people. It is certain, at all events,
that the Scottish statute book contains many Acts, tending to secure the
liberty as well as to foster the well-being of the subject, which even yet
may stand as models of legislative wisdom ... In their benevolent care of
the poor, both from starvation and the litigious oppression of the rich, in
the protection of the subject from arbitrary imprisonment, in the
recognition of the right of all prisoners to be defended by counsel, in the
establishment of an excellent system of popular education, in the humane
restriction of the death penalty, the old Scottish Parliament had anticipated
legislation which came to the people of England more than a century
after the Union.[42]

The 1884 Reform Act gave the vote to men over 21 and so
enfranchised the male working class. Progress towards Home Rule
now became possible. In the same decade the Scottish Home Rule
Association was founded and the Scottish Liberal Party adopted for
the first time a policy of Home Rule for Scotland. In response to
increasing discontent with the treatment of Scotland, the Government
re-established the Office of Secretary of State for Scotland. Between
1886 and 1900 seven Scottish Home Rule motions were presented to
the House of Commons and a majority of Scottish members voted
for all but the first of them. These political developments were
accompanied by a resurgence in literature and the other arts, the
Scottish National Portrait Gallery, the Scottish text Society (for the
publication of early Scottish literature) and the Scottish History
Society were formed. Stevenson wrote *Kidnapped* and *The Master
of Ballantrae* and much of his poetry in Scots. William McTaggart
was painting and Hamish MacCunn composing. By 1895, Patrick
Geddes was able to write in his periodical, Evergreen, (a deliberate
echo of Allan Ramsay's revival of poetry in Scots in the 18th century)
of a Scottish renaissance. In spite of the interruption of two world
wars, this cultural and political revival has continued to the present
with a confidence and insistence that could not be ignored.

One of the worst consequences of the Union was that it prevented
for nearly three hundred years the development of Scottish society

References

1 Sir Walter Scott, *Letters*, ed. H J C Grierson, 12 Vols. (London 1932-38), Vol IX, p437.

2 Sir Walter Scott, *The Letters of Malachi Malagrowther* (1826), *ed* P H Scott, (Edinburgh 1981), p9.

3 *Ibid*. p4.

4 Linda Colley, *Britons: Forging the Nation 1707-1837* (London 1992), p5.

5 Richard Finlay, 'Caledonia or North Britain' in *Image and Identity*, ed. D Broun, R J Finlay and M Lynch (Edinburgh 1998), pp151-2.

6 *Ibid*. p150.

7 Tom Nairn in *Scottish Affairs* (Special Issue), 'Understanding Constitutional Change' (Edinburgh 1998), p26.

8 Linda Colley, *Journal of British Studies*, Vol 31, No 4, Oct 1992, pp325-6.

9 Michael Lynch, *Scotland: A New History,* (London 1991), pXIV.

10 Linda Colley, op. cit.,p130.

11 Graham Walker, 'Varieties of Scottish Protestant Identity' in *Scotland in the 20th Century*, ed. T M Devine and R J Finlay (Edinburgh 1996), p251.

12 Elizabeth Hay, *Sambo Sahib* (Edinburgh 1981), p111.

13 In the conclusion of *A Union of Multiple Identities*, ed. Laurence Brocklin and David Eastwood, (Manchester 1997), pp194-5.

14 Tacitus, *The Agricola*, translated by H. Mottingly, (Harmondsworth 1980), pp72-3.

15 David Hume, *Letters*, ed. J Greig (Oxford 1932), Vol II, pp170-1.

16 Michael Hechter, *Internal Colonialism*, (London 1975), pp73, 81.

17 C J Watson, 'The Novels of Neil Gunn' in *Literature of the North,* ed. David Hewitt and Michael Spiller, (Aberdeen 1983), p140.

18 Trevor Royle in *Scotland on Sunday,* 'Spectrum', 26th April 1998, p22.

19 See, for example, Cairns Craig, *Out of History* (Edinburgh 1996), p12 and passim.

20 By a speaker at a conference in Inverness in April 1999.

21 Lindsay Paterson, *The Anatomy of Modern Scotland,* (Edinburgh, 1994), pp5,73.

22 R H Campbell, *Scotland Since 1707* (Edinburgh 1971), p9.

23 Lord Cockburn, *quoted* in *Lord Cockburn: A Bicentenary Commemoration* (Edinburgh 1979), p94.

24 Lord Cockburn, *Journal* (Edinburgh 1874), Vol II, p30.

25 Eric Linklater, *The Lion and the Unicorn* (London 1935), p26. Edwin Muir *Scottish Journey* (1935), (edition of 1979, Edinburgh), p25.

26 Edwin Muir, *Scottish Journey* (1935), *op.cit.,* p3.

27 William Ferguson, *Edinburgh History of Scotland: Vol. IV, 1688-Present* (Edinburgh 1968) p.319.

28 Lord Rosebery, quoted in Richard J. Finlay, *A Partnership for Good?* (Edinburgh 1997), p42.

29 Christopher Harvie, *No Gods and Precious Few Heroes: Twentieth Century Scotland* (1981), Vol. 8 of *New History of Scotland* (edition of 1998, Edinburgh), pvii.

30 Ferguson, op. cit., p320.

31 Paterson, op. cit., p.46.

32 A V Dicey and R S Rait, *Thoughts on the Union* (London 1920), p.362.

33 Sydney and Olive Checkland, *Industry and Ethos: Scotland 1832-1914,* Vol. 7 of *The New History of Scotland,* (London 1984), p112.

34 George Davie, *The Democratic Intellect* (Edinburgh 1961), p106.

35 Allan Massie in *Jock Tamson's Bairns*, ed. Trevor Royle, (London 1977), p69.

36 *The Letters of Robert Burns*, ed. J De Lancey Ferguson, (Oxford 1931), Vol II, p143.

37 Colley, *Britons: Forging the Nation 1707-1837, op. cit.,* p.350.

38 Colin Kidd, *Subverting Scotland's Past* (Cambridge 1993), p209.

39 Michael Dyer, *Men of Property and Intelligence: The Scottish Electoral System Prior to 1884* (Aberdeen 1996), p4.

40 Michael Fry, *The Dundas Despotism* (Edinburgh 1992), p381.

41 An extract of a translation of George Buchanan's *De Jure Regni Apud Scotos* is in *Scotland: An Unwon Cause*, ed. P H Scott (Edinburgh 1987), pp468-9.

42 James Mackinnon, *The Union of England and Scotland* (London 1896), pp468-9; extract in *Scotland: An Unwon Cause, op. cit.,* pp36.

CHAPTER 6

The End of Empire and of Britishness

As we have seen in the previous chapter, Scots generally for more than a century before 1945 embraced not Britain but the British Empire. The justification for the Union and the British state was the scope which the Empire offered to Scotland for commercial, career and philanthropic ambitions. That concealed, but did not prevent, increasing discontent with what was widely seen as the unfair treatment of Scotland itself. The end of the Empire was a radical change. If the Empire had been the justification for the Union, what justification was there when the Empire no longer existed?

"Imperial Britain <u>was</u> Britain", David Marquand has written, "Empire was not an optional extra for the British; it was their reason for being British as opposed to English or Scots or Welsh. Deprived of empire and plunged into Europe, 'Britain' had no meaning."[1] Towards the end of her book, *Britons*, Linda Colley says: "No more can Britons reassure themselves of their distinct and privileged identity by contrasting themselves with impoverished Europeans (real or imaginary), or by exercising authority over manifestly alien peoples. God has ceased to be British, and Providence no longer smiles."[2] In an essay she quotes a Welsh historian, Owyn Williams, who wrote in 1979: "The British nation and the British state are clearly entering a process of dissolution, into Europe or the mid-Atlantic or a post-imperial fog. Britain has begun its long march out of history."[3]

Between 1947 and 1990, fifty former British colonies became independent countries. This was a process which British Governments, both Conservative and Labour, carried out smoothly and rapidly. All the former colonies welcomed independence enthusiastically; none have any desire to return to rule from London. British Governments deserve credit for this vast expansion of self-determination and democracy; but for more than a century they have resisted the application of the same right to Scotland. In a television programme in March 1998, Ludovic Kennedy said that he was present to report for the BBC at scores of hand-over ceremonies in former British colonies where the Union flag was lowered and the flag of the newly independent country was raised. "I started to think", he said, "if these little places, and some of them very small and very poor, can have self-government, why can't Scotland?"[4]

The end of the Empire has exposed confusion and uncertainties over the meaning of Britishness. This is particularly acute in England, where people seem to have difficulty in making a distinction between England and Britain, and habitually use the two terms interchangeably. In Scotland we have always been alert to the distinction. It is true that for a time in the 19th century some Scots, even at times R. L. Stevenson, made some attempt to accept England as an inclusive description. Nowadays most of us feel that this was a concession too far.

There is a wide measure of agreement that one reason for this uncertainty over the meaning of Britishness is that Britain, as an artificial political construction, has never evolved into a cultural identity capable of supplanting those of England, Scotland, Wales or Ireland. This may, of course, have simply been because the national characters of the component parts, evolved over centuries, were too strongly embedded to be displaced by a political expedient imposed on top of them. The alternative explanation is that British Governments were never interested in trying to make such a change. David Eastwood and other English historians in a book which I quoted in the last chapter, *A Union of Multiple Identities*, published in 1997, offer an explanation:

> British Unionism rested, fundamentally, on an extension of the domain of the English Crown and the English Parliament....Political discourse was broadly built around the assumption that Parliament, not the people, was sovereign. As long as the inhabitants of the British Isles accepted the very English idea that change could occur legitimately only if

sanctioned by the British Parliament, there was a limited need to foster unity by State-sponsored acculturation. It may have been naive of the British ruling élite to assume that the belief in parliamentary sovereignty would always pertain - after all, the Americans had already found a way out of the ideological straitjacket - but the definite pervasiveness of the idea helps to explain why there was little British interest in the positive promotion of Britishness." [5]

The importance attached in England to the idea of parliamentary sovereignty also explains the frantic efforts of Tony Blair in 1996 to claw back the commitment to the sovereignty of the Scottish people which the Scottish Labour members of Parliament (except one) made by signing the Claim of Right in March 1989. Again inconsistently, the Devolution White Paper, *Scotland's Parliament* says quite bluntly: "The UK Parliament is and will remain sovereign."[6] The Scotland Act, which restores the Scottish Parliament, has the sweeping provision in clause 28(7) that it "does not affect the power of the Parliament of the United Kingdom to make laws for Scotland. " These provisions are presumably inserted to gratify the adherents of "the very English idea"; but the fact is that both the existence of the Scottish Parliament and of European legislation very substantially erode the sovereignty of the Westminster Parliament.

There have been other more cynical, or perhaps more realistic, explanations of the failure of the British state to develop "a genuinely British identity." This phrase is used by Colin Kidd in his book, *Subverting Scottish History,* published in 1993. This is a sustained argument that Scottish Whig historians made Scotland a "historyless nation" by rejecting the Scottish past because only English history could explain British institutions. (a reflection, I think, more of the powerlessness of Scotland after the Union than of any inadequacy in Scottish historical precedents). In spite of his line of argument, Kidd agrees that there was "a lack of English commitment to a British idea which was more than either an alternative name for England or a euphemism which disguised the nature of the English core's imperial relationships with her assorted peripheries." [7]

Cairns Craig in *Out of History* (1996) argues that England is so confident of the centrality of its own cultural tradition that it simply assimilates any work from the periphery that it happens to like and ignores the rest. Similarly English history is regarded as the essential historical process and Scottish and Irish issues are only relevant "when they destructively intrude" into the English narrative. English history is not interested in the multi-national character of the British state, but in class which extends over boundaries. 'Class relations have provided the medium through which English society has been able to incorporate the societies on its margins."[8]

Kenneth Lunn, Reader in Social History at the University of Portsmouth, is even blunter in a paper published in 1996:

> The use of the term 'English' as a synonym for 'British' is more than just a slovenly application of the word. It represents a series of assumptions about the natural rights of England to speak for Britain and, by the imposed silence, the inability of Welsh, Irish and Scottish voices to challenge effectively those assumptions. It reproduces the imperial philosophy in which the mother country represented the greater whole.[9]

I think that Lunn's remarks are an honest reflection of the way in which many, perhaps most, people in England feel. This fact, and all the other theories taken together (for they all say very much the same thing) help to explain not only the failure of Britain to become an all-embracing identity, but also the futility of the Scottish efforts to persuade the English that the Treaty of Union meant what it said. In other words, that it was a partnership in which the new entity, Great Britain, replaced both England and Scotland. Scotland tried hard in the imperial age to play this game and even used North Britain as its postal address. It had some significance as long as the Empire existed, but that disappeared when the Empire collapsed. Scotland tried, but the English were not interested. The conception of Britain has been exposed as little more than a deception, a trick of propaganda, to conceal an English take-over.

The Empire is not the only prop of Britishness which has disappeared or greatly diminished. The Union is no longer needed to safeguard the northern border of England or to conduct an anti-French and anti-Catholic crusade. Respect for the British Parliament and the monarchy are no longer what they were. Increasingly in this century, and especially under Thatcher and Blair, the Parliament has become, not an expression of democracy, but a device for the exercise of prime ministerial power. The prestige of the monarchy, probably less in any case in Scotland than in England, has been tarnished. Andrew Fletcher said that as an institution it was as illogical as a hereditary professorship would be. The illogicality remains and so does its embodiment of the principle of inherited privilege which is at variance both with our egalitarian instincts and the spirit of the age. Little now remains of the structure of Britishness, except residual habit, the residue of decades of propaganda, the wishful thinking of Unionist politicians and the BBC. The last of these, which is strongly Anglo-centric, is still a powerful voice. It has been described as the cement which holds the Union together. This is, no doubt, why the Scotland Act proposes to leave the regulation of broadcasting in the hands of the Westminster Parliament.

Meanwhile, what has been happening inside Scotland itself during the 20th century? There is a wide measure of agreement among economic and social historians that the story is one of decline, especially in comparison to other industrial countries in western Europe. David McCrone has drawn attention to the research of John Scott and Michael Hughes, published in 1980, which "charted the radical transformation in Scottish business this century, from a self-confident, locally controlled economy, to a weakened, externally dependent one."[10] T. M. Devine in *Scotland in the 20th Century*: "In 1914 Scotland was a global economic power; yet by the 1990s the country's key industries were predominantly foreign-owned. In the early 1970s nearly sixty per cent of manufacturing employment was in plants whose ownership lay outside Scotland. Even more significantly only fourteen per cent of the five fastest growing sectors were Scottish controlled."[11] Christopher Harvie in his history of 20th century *Scotland, No Gods and Precious Few Heroes*, says that he has had to record "Scotland's industrial stagnation and eventual decline." He denies that it is contradictory to this that living standards, for part of the population at least, have risen:

> This advance has been common to all West European nations, and in most of them has been much more rapid than in Scotland.....The expansion in well-being (in Scotland) has been recent, and looks like being short-lived, while the industrial base remains in decay. It has, moreover, benefited only 77 per cent of those born in Scotland since 1911, the rest having emigrated. In 1911 Sweden's population was only 16 per cent greater than Scotland's; by 1970 the margin had widened to 55 per cent. Swedish gross domestic product per head was barely half that of Scotland in 1911: about £32 against about £62. By 1970 it was £1,812 against £709. By such standards, Scotland's twentieth-century performance has been grim.[12]

Harvie's reference to comparative population growth makes an important point. Adam Smith said that "the most decisive mark of the prosperity of any country is the increase of the number of its inhabitants."[13] Again, since population tends to increase almost everywhere, we have to look at it in comparative terms. By this standard, the Scottish decline has been dramatic. At the time of the Union in 1707, the population of Scotland was about 18% of that of Great Britain; in the census of 1991 it was only 9.2%, and it is forecast by the Central Statistical Office that it will sink to 7 6% by 2031. Scotland is one of very few countries where the population is actually declining. Between 1931 and 1991 it declined at a rate of 0.34% per year and in 1991 it fell below 5 million for the first time since 1931. Clearly, if any part of Britain has benefited from the Union, it is not Scotland.

There are two reasons for this decline in population. The birth rate has fallen since the beginning of the century and there is now a near balance between it and the death rate. In addition, there has been a massive loss of population through emigration: nearly 2 million people between 1900 and 1991. This reflects dissatisfaction with economic conditions in Scotland and, in particular, a shortage of employment opportunities. The "branch plant" economy which Scotland has become has meant a loss of senior jobs in management, legal, advertising and accountancy services and research. Rationalisation on a British scale has also meant the removal from Scotland of innumerable functions, including such things as the handling of telephone accounts, the issue of driving and television licences and even enquiries about train timings. For these reasons many of the emigrants are highly educated or skilled and most of them are young. Two thirds of them between 1889/90 and 1991/92 were between 15 and 39. The serious implications of this for the future of the country are obvious. It is what Edwin Muir had in mind when he said that his main impression about Scotland was it was "gradually being emptied of its population, its spirit, its wealth, industry, art, intellect and innate character."[14]

Many of the achievements of Scottish industry in the past were impressive. One sixth of the world production of ships in 1913, for example, were launched from yards on the Clyde. But this was accompanied "by poor living standards, enduring poverty and almost uniquely poor housing."[15] We continue to suffer from this legacy. "By 1989 almost half a million people in Scotland were receiving income support ... Scotland has long had a history of chronic ill health, sustaining death rates from heart disease and lung cancer amongst the highest in the world as well as a relatively high infant mortality rate." These quotations come from a study of Scotland in the 20th century by an economic historian, C. H. Lee. His conclusion is: "Such a society is locked, by a variety of mechanisms, into a cycle of decline."[16]

It is a reflection of the high prevalence of poverty, and therefore of deplorable health standards, that Government spending on social and health services is higher in Scotland than in England. This makes up most of the so-called "identifiable" expenditure, that is on the items which the Government choses to identify; but that does not necessarily mean that total Government expenditure per head is higher in Scotland. In fact, on such matters as civil service pay, defence research and procurement, transport subsidies and mortgage tax relief, most of the expenditure is in London and the South East of England.

Scotland is a country which has many strengths and advantages: in natural resources, once coal and iron, now oil; in a temperate climate, plentiful water, much good agricultural land; in coastal waters with good anchorages and stocks of fish; in its ability to feed itself; in its attractiveness to tourists; in its vibrant and distinctive culture; above all in its intelligent, educated, resourceful and inventive population. It has made a contribution to civilisation out of all proportion to its size. "All nations," the poet Douglas Dunn has written, "can point to their geniuses in may realms of human endeavour; but for a country of its size, Scotland's contribution is almost disturbing in its scale."[17]

You would expect to find a country with these qualities to be a model of prosperity, achievement and social justice. Instead you find a disastrous loss of population and levels of poverty, poor health and bad housing which are about the worst among advanced industrial countries. There must be something fundamentally wrong about the system of government which produces such a deplorable result and such a waste of potential. C. H. Lee says: "Many studies of British economic policy in the twentieth century have depicted it as characterised by a mixture of folly and incompetence. Scotland has suffered from that malaise."[18] In fact, it has suffered disproportionately because the Government naturally favours the areas of greater population close to London, and that is also the tendency of commercial firms with their head offices in the same area. Andrew Fletcher was right to predict that the effect of the Union would be to "draw the riches and government of the three kingdoms to the south-east corner of this island."[19]

Scotland is conspicuously less successful and less prosperous than the small independent countries of western Europe and the gap between us is widening. By GDP per head, the most prosperous country in Europe is Luxembourg, followed by Switzerland, Norway, Denmark and Austria. All of them are about the same size as Scotland or smaller, and most of them are less well provided with natural resources. Are they more successful because they are independent and Scotland is not? As far as I know, no one has suggested any other explanation. It is not surprising that the Scottish people increasingly draw the obvious conclusion.

References

[1] David Marquand, *quoted* by Murray Ritchie in *The Herald*, 16th December 1996, from *Britain's European Question: The Issues for Ireland*, ed. Paul Gillespie. (Institute of European Affairs)

[2] Linda Colley, *Britons: Forging the Nation 1707-1837* (London 1992) p374.

[3] Linda Colley, *Journal of British Studies* Volume 31, October 1992 pp328-9

[4] Ludovic Kennedy in a television programme on Channel 4 on 22nd March 1998.

[5] In *A Union of Multiple Identities*, ed. Laurence Brocklin and David Eastwood, (Manchester 1997), pp196, 203.

[6] *Scotland's Parliament*, The Scottish Office, Cm. 3658, July 1997, pX.

[7] Colin Kidd, *Subverting Scotland's Past* (Cambridge 1996), p272.

[8] Cairns Craig, *Out of History* (Edinburgh 1996), pp101,104.

[9] Kenneth Lunn, 'Reconsidering Britishness' in *Nation and Identity in Contemporary Europe*, ed. Brian Jenkins and Spyros A. Sofos, (London 1996), p87.

[10] David McCrone, *Understanding Scotland: The Sociology of a Stateless Nation*, (London 1992), p133.

11 T M Devine, in *Scotland in the 20th Century*, ed. T M Devine and R J Finlay, (Edinburgh 1996), p4.

12 Christopher Harvie, *No Gods and Precious Few Heroes: Twentieth Century Scotland* (1981), Vol. 8 of *New History of Scotland* (edition of 1998, Edinburgh), p.VII.

13 Adam Smith, *The Wealth of Nations* (1776), Everman's Library edition, (London 1971), Vol.1, p62.

14 Edwin Muir *Scottish Journey* (1935), (Edinburgh 1979), p3.

15 C H Lee, *Scotland and the United Kingdom* (Manchester 1995), pp47-48.

16 *Ibid*. pp72,75.

17 Douglas Dunn, Introduction to *Scotland, An Anthology* (London 1992), p6.

18 Lee, *op.cit.*, p215.

19 Andrew Fletcher of Saltoun, 'Account of a Conversation' in *Selected Political Writings and Speeches of Andrew Fletcher of Saltoun*, ed. David Daiches, (Edinburgh 1979), p135.

CHAPTER 7

Return to Europe

Scottish members of Parliament continued to put forward Home Rule motions in Parliament in the early years of the 20th century. They were supported by a majority of members from Scotland but made no progress because the Government invariably declined to allow parliamentary time. In 1912 the Prime Minister, Herbert Asquith, appeared to promise legislation, but no action was taken and the first World War intervened. The campaign for a Scottish Parliament resumed after the War, which had after all been fought in defence of the principle of self determination. The Scottish Council of the Labour Party in September 1919 adopted a resolution which demanded the application of this principle to Scotland. One of the speakers in the debate, Hugh Lyon, said that there was "an urgent need for Scots Home Rule ... They would not have real social reconstruction in Scotland while they were held back by England. Freedom of government was necessary for Scotland in order that progress would be made in harmony with the aspirations of the people."[1] The belief that social reform in Scotland was being held back by English conservatism was not confined to the Labour Party. A Liberal speaker in the House of Commons in August 1919, for instance, said "There is not one single item in the whole programme of radicalism or social reform today, which if Scotland had power to pass laws, would not have been carried out a quarter of a century ago."[2]

These Scottish Liberal and Labour spokesmen may well have been sincere, but they were members of British parties and the English majority and leadership of these parties had different ideas and different priorities. They were reluctant to commit themselves to measures in which English voters had no interest and might resent. "I tell you straight", a Labour member is reported to have said in

1926, "that the Labour MPs have received instructions to do nothing
to imperil the future prospects of the Party holding office at
Westminster."[3] That was always likely to be the attitude of the
leadership of a British party. Supporters of Home Rule had relied on
these parties to achieve legislation: but after repeated disappointment
and frustration, many of them decided that only a purely Scottish
party with a Scottish Parliament as its main objective was likely to
achieve results. Two such parties were formed and they were
amalgamated in 1934 as the Scottish National Party.

Progress was at first slow. The British electoral system is not
kind to a new party, especially when it has to rely on its membership
for funds and when established voting habits and most of the media
are opposed to it. Robert McIntyre won the first SNP parliamentary
seat at a by-election in 1945, but it was not until the 1960s that the
SNP began to win sufficient support to present a serious challenge
to the British parties. From then onwards, the need for a Scottish
party became obvious because it was only the advance of the SNP
which provoked the other parties into movement towards
constitutional change. Each important step has been a response to an
SNP advance. Winnie Ewing's victory for the SNP in Hamilton in
1967 was followed by Heath's Declaration of Perth (in which he
committed the Conservative Party to an elected Assembly for
Scotland) and also by the appointment by the Labour Government of
a Royal Commission on the constitution. The success of the SNP in
winning 11 seats and 42 second places in a General Election in 1974
led to the London leadership of the Labour Party insisting on the re-
adoption by the Scottish Labour Party of the policy of Home Rule
(now called Devolution) which it had abandoned in 1958. Jim Sillars'
victory in Govan in 1988 was followed by the decision of the Labour
Party to join the Constitutional Convention. It was hardly possible
for the SNP to do so because the declared purpose of the Convention
was to strengthen the Union. I do not propose to give an account of
the tortuous events which after so much time and effort eventually

led to the Referendum of 11th September 1997 and therefore to the Scotland Act which will restore the Scottish Parliament in 1999. There are many excellent books which do this already.[4] But I should like to comment on the attitude of the British parties to the Union and to constitutional change. For a time in the 1970s all four of the major parties were in favour, in theory at least, of a measure of constitutional change. The three British parties were, however, committed at the same time to maintaining the Union. The policy of the Liberal Party and its successor in this matter has been consistent for over a century. The attitude of the Conservatives and Labour has been much more convoluted and variable. "In the early 1970s the Conservatives had three policies in as many years, favouring at successive annual conferences first an indirect assembly, then no assembly, then a directly elected one." [5] That was not the end of it. When Margaret Thatcher became Conservative leader in 1974 she at first embraced devolution as a "top priority" as she said in a speech in Glasgow.[6] Then she became and remained a resolute opponent. The former Conservative Prime Minister, Lord Home, appeared on television a few days before the vote on the Referendum of 1979. He approved of the principle of devolution, but called for a 'no' vote on the Labour Act on the grounds that it was too weak and did not provide for tax-raising powers. He promised that a Conservative Government would introduce a better Act. They were then in power for 18 years, but made no such move. Their most frequently repeated argument against the Labour proposal in 1997 was that it did include tax-raising powers, although they were of a very limited kind. For the whole period of Conservative Government they argued fiercely against any form of Scottish Parliament or Assembly. After the emphatic vote in September 1997 for the Scottish Parliament they have accepted it. In opposition they are quite prepared to "play the Scottish card" and accuse the Labour Government of London control and Anglicisation, just as their predecessors accused the Whigs in the early nineteenth century.

Within the Labour Party there is also a Unionist tradition. This was not so apparent in the early years of the party when they were enthusiastic Home Rulers. When their first MPs left for London they promised that they would soon be back in a Scottish Parliament. This spirit faded after the Second World War when the party emphasised the ideology of central (which meant London) economic planning and central ownership of industry and utilities. Their nationalisation of the railways and of coal, steel and shipbulding was a major part of the loss of Scottish control of Scottish industry. In the 1950 General Election, Labour for the first time had no commitment to Scottish Home Rule and it formally ceased to be part of their policy in 1958. Only the intervention of the London leadership brought the Scottish party back to it in 1974. In the Referendum of 1979, although it was held on the basis of Labour legislation, the party in Scotland campaigned on both sides and their activists mostly stayed at home.

The experience of the long period of Conservative rule under Thatcher and Major changed many minds. At every General Election the Conservatives were soundly rejected by the Scottish electorate, but that did not stop them imposing highly unpopular policies on Scotland. This persuaded many people that the British state, with the constitution as it stood, was undemocratic and unacceptable. Many of the doubters, who had hampered the Labour Party at the time of the 1979 Referendum had become enthusiasts for a Scottish Parliament by 1997. Opinion poll evidence shows that many Labour voters favour independence, and a few of their MPs may have leanings in that direction. Their leadership, both in Scotland and England, is however firmly Unionist. They seldom refer to the Scottish Parliament without immediately adding the caveat, "within the United Kingdom."

Both the Conservative Party, during its devolutionary phases, and the Labour Party since 1974 have regarded the policy of a devolved and limited Parliament primarily as a tactic to counter the

appeal of the SNP. They have always said that the purpose of
Devolution is to strengthen, not weaken, the Union. The belief, or
the hope, was the Scots would be satisfied with the half-way house
and lose any desire to aspire to anything more, at least for some
years. George Robertson, who was Labour Shadow Secretary of
State for Scotland before the Election of 1997, used to say that a
devolved Scottish Parliament would "kill the SNP stone dead." It
should have been obvious that the effect was likely to be the opposite.
The prospect, and still more the existence, of the Scottish Parliament,
and the election campaign before it, would focus attention on Scottish
issues. The arguments for a Scottish parliament lead logically to the
case for independence. If it is desirable for the Scots to have control
of their own affairs, why should they be hedged in with so many
restrictions? Why should they not be free to make their own decisions
about taxation and Government spending or about the presence of
nuclear weapons on their soil? Why should they not participate in
European decision making? Why should Scotland have a lesser status
and less power than Denmark, Ireland or Luxembourg? The strange
thing is that Labour seem to have believed their own propaganda and
to be genuinely surprised by the surge in support for the SNP and for
independence.

But why is the Labour Party Unionist? It used to be said that they
had no hope of power at Westminster without the Scottish seats; but
after the Election of 1997, this is true no longer. Of course, British
parties inevitably think in British terms and party discipline (now
much stronger in the Labour Party than ever before) restrains dissident
voices from Scotland. Labour now longer places its faith in central
planning and nationalisation, but some remnant of left-wing thought
clings to vague internationalist ideas. There seems to be an idea that
London control is more respectable from this point of view than self-
determination for Scotland, which can be described as "narrow
nationalism." Strangely enough, those who take this view are
generally in favour of self-determination almost everywhere else, as

in the dissolution of the British Empire or the Soviet Union. Perhaps Labour activists and MPs are mostly opposed to independence and the SNP for the simple reason that tbe two parties are in competition for the same seats. We have to remember that politics are not only about ideas, but about careers.

Labour leaders usually speak as if they thought that the Union was so self-evidently a good thing that it requires no justification. If pressed, they use such arguments as the following: we do not want to separate people in Scotland from their friends and relatives in England or create barriers to trade; we want to spare Scotland the expense of its own defence forces and embasssies abroad; we do not want to lose the "identifiable" expenditure; Britain has a stronger voice in Europe as part of Britain than Scotland would have on its own; we do not want to create tensions and ill-will between Scotland and England. These are arguments on a fairly trivial level, appealing more to an instinctive nervousness of change than to any rational reality. Most of them ignore the effects of membership of the European Union.

Let me take the last of the arguments first. Certainly, tension between Scotland and England is to be deplored, but it is much more likely to arise when Westmister has the right to intervene in large areas of Scottish affairs. Control of the purse strings is the ultimate control and the Scotland Act leaves that almost entirely in the hands of Westmister. Also Scotland will have no right to make its own case, or to make its own contribution to decision making in the European Union. All of these are likely to be sources of discontent and disagreement. The relationship between Scotland and England would be far more co-operative and friendly if Scotland was free to make all its own decisions and we were both members of the European Union in our own right. It is the humiliation and frustration of subordination that is liable to cause tension and ill-will.

The European Union makes a radical difference. We are no longer in a British market of 40 million and a British economy, but in a

European market of 290 million and a global economy. Inside the European Union there is complete freedom of movement of people, money and goods. With the enlargement of membership within the next few years, virtually the whole of Europe west of Russia will be included,with the exception, perhaps temporary, of Norway and Switzerland. Most of the new member countries will be of about the same size as Scotland or smaller. The smaller states, with many common interests, will be in an even larger majority than they are at present. As I mentioned in the previous chapter, the present small member nations are among the prosperous in the world. All the pointers throughout Europe suggest that "this is the age of the small nations", as Murray Ritchie said in an article in *The Herald* on 8th April 1998. Scotland is a small nation with greater potential than most, but it cannot take its proper place with the others until it achieves independence.

The advantages of the small nation were discussed at an international symposium held in 1995 to celebrate the 400th anniversary of the University of Uppsala. Philippe Schmitter of Stanford University said that even the smallest European states, such a Lichtenstein and Luxembourg were remarkably successful and that the comparative advantage of Europe lay in the great diversity of its component parts. Johan Olsen of Oslo University said that many of the smaller nations had a good historical record in "democratic development, peaceful co-existence, prosperity, welfare, equality between social classes, districts and gender, life expectancy, cultural developments, and ecological consciousness." (You might say in everything that matters.) Olsen suggested that one reason for the success of small nations was their adaptability, derived from their experience in adapting to external events. [7] There is an obvious similarity between these observations and the ideas expressed by philosophers of the Scottish Enlightenment such as Fletcher, Hume, Millar and Ferguson.[8]

The history of this century has been marked by two apparently contradictory tendencies. The first is the emergence of international organisations, such as the United Nations and the European Union, in which member states pool part of their sovereignty. The other is the division of empires and multi-national states into their compnent parts. In this century the Austro-Hungarian, British, Dutch, French and Portuguese empires and the Soviet Union have dissolved. Scores of new states and of long suppressed or absorbed nations, most of them small, have become independent. Once again, the exception is Scotland, which is extraordinary when you consider how well provided we are, both historically and at present, with the attributes of statehood.

The two tendencies of international co-operation and the emergence of new states are less contradictory than they appear at first sight. This is because the international organisations make the world a safer and more congenial place for small countries. Their tendency is to curb the power of the large states and enhance the influence of the small. Paradoxically, the effect of the pooling of sovereignty is to make the small nations more secure in their own sovereignty. Even when there is a weighted voting system (as there is in the European Union), the fundamental ethos of international organisations is that all member states, as members of the club as it were, have equal rights; that account must be taken of the interests and views of all members; that there are rules which all, even the largest and most powerful, must respect. In the past, small states were often at the mercy of their larger neighbours who could dictate to them, as happened to Scotland in the Union of 1707. There are now curbs on the rule of the jungle. The point has been made by a Danish Prime Minister, Poul Schulter:

I feel today a lot more powerful than a Danish Prime Minister would have felt years ago. Why? Because under all circumstances, this is a rather small neighbouring country to Germany and the strong German economy. In the old days, we just had to accept any step taken in the German economy, and it had consequences to us. Nowadays, my ministers and I, myself, take part in the Council meetings in Europe. We have influence, and we have a lot more more influence than is fair, considering that we are such a small nation.[9]

This is the great difference between the Anglo-Scottish Union of 1707 and the European Union. In 1707 the Scottish Parliament was in effect absorbed into the English, now called British, Parliament, in which the Scottish members were a small and impotent minority. Under the English doctrine of parliamentary sovereignty, this Parliament was then free to legislate as it pleased without having to take Scottish views into account. We had none of the rights which the rules of the European Union gives to its member states. But a state has to be a member before this applies. A country which is not independent has no international existence and no right to have its views and interests considered, either in the European Union or anywhere else.

In this respect, there has been a retreat from the White Paper of July 1997, *Scotland's Parliament*, which was the subject of the referendum, and the Scotland Act, which purports to implement it. The White Paper in paragraph 5.6 said that "in appropriate cases, Scottish Executive Ministers could speak for the United Kingdom in Councils." Thus did not give them a right to express a specifically Scottish point of view, but only an agreed United Kingdom position. Even this very limited right has been withdrawn in the Act. It makes no such concession, but merely reserves international relations, including those with the European Union, to Westminster. The Scotland Act will leave Scotland without an international identity or any right to defend its interests or views in international organisations. Unionists argue that Scotland has a stronger voice in Europe as part of Britain than it would have on its own. In fact, this so-called stronger voice is really no voice at all, especially when Scottish interests are at variance with those of England. Since Britain has shown itself to be a reluctant and difficult member of the European Union, often in a minority of one and more often than not on the losing side, it cannot rely on popularity for influence. Such claim as it has to an influential voice depends on the system of qualified majority voting in the Council of Ministers. This is an allocation of votes between member countries roughly in proportion to their population, except that the smaller countries have more votes than strict proportionality would allow. The United Kingdom, France, Germany and Italy, as the larger countries, each have 10 votes. Others have a lesser number between 8 and 2. Scotland would fall into the group of Ireland, Denmark and Finland, each of which have 3. A decision requires a majority of 62. It follows that even if the four larger countries vote the same way, they still require the support of a number of the smaller ones. This is a system which ensures that the small countries, which are about to increase in number, already have an important part in the process of decision making. They are in a far stronger position on their own than they would be as part of a larger neighbour, as a former Irish Prime Minister, Garret Fitzgerald, has pointed out:

> If we had not been independent during the first half of this century, and if we had joined the Community (as the European Union was then called) as part of a recalcitrant and unenthusiastic United Kingdom, we would have had neither the capacity to secure our interests within the Community nor an opportunity to express our personality and make our own distinctive, if necessarily modest, contribution to the development of this new political structure for Europe.[10]

When Mary Robinson, then President of Ireland, was on a visit to Scotland in June 1992 she said that membership of the Community had brought a "great sense of liberation. We have become more sure of our own Irish identity in the context of being equal partners in Europe. It meant we no longer simply define ourselves in terms of our relationship with Britain. We are Irish, but we are also European."[11] The relevance of this Irish experience to Scotland is very obvious. We too need our own membership of the European Union to secure our interests" and "express our personality." It is widely recognised that Ireland has benefited greatly by her status of "independence in Europe." Iain MacWhirter in *The Scotsman* on 12th March 1998 suggested that Ireland was a model of what Scotland could become:

> Ireland, which used to be regarded by Unionists as a backward, in-bred, agrarian theocracy, is now talked of as a mini-tiger economy of Europe ... and a cultural icon for the world. Ireland has done this by exploiting the opportunities presented by Europe ... Indeed, it is not too hard to envisage a future in which it is Britain which looks backward - stuck in an English nationalist time-warp, left behind in Europe, an unappreciated lapdog of American presidents.

Unionists used to argue that an independent Scotland, but not the rest of the United Kingdom apparently, would have to re-apply for membership of the European Union and might not be accepted. They seem to have abandoned this argument in the face of authoritative opinion to the contrary, that of Emile Noel, the former Secretary General of the European Commisssion, for example:

> There is no precedent and no provision for the expulsion of a member state, therefore Scottish independence would create two new member states out of one. They would have equal status with each other and the other 11 states. The remainder of the United Kingdom would not be in a more powerful position than Scotland ... Anyone who is attacking the claim in respect of one country is attacking it in respect of the other. It is not possible to divide the cases.[12]

There remain two further Unionist arguments, those about the cost of separate defence and diplomatic representation and about the loss of an alleged subsidy in the form of the "identified expenditure." There is no reason why Scotland could not afford a realistic defence force in accordance with her size and needs and appropriate diplomatic representation. Other countries of a comparable size do both of these things perfectly well. We should probably have to spend less than we do at present in contributing our share of the inflated cost of maintaining both defence and diplomatic establishments on a scale which reflects British aspirations to retain the trappings of the great power status which she has long lost in reality. In particular, we should not have to contribute to the enormous cost of the submarines with nuclear weapons on the Clyde. Apart fom the cost, these weapons are immoral, useless and liable to catastrophic accident. The fact that they are inflicted on us, whether we like it or not, and most people in Scotland do not, is one of the worst of the present damaging and humiliating effects of the Union. As with the disproportionate burden of military casualties in past wars, Scotland is made to suffer a major part of the risk in upholding British ambitions of power.

On the vexed question of the alleged subsidy, there seems to be little doubt that in the 19th century Scotland contributed more in taxation to the British Treasury than it received back in expediture. In this century, the question has become more complex. Expenditure on the items which the Government chooses to identify, (mainly education and health and social services), hardly existed before this century. Higher expenditure on these per head in Scotland reflect the costs involved in the wider dispersal of the population; but, and to a much larger extent, greater poverty and the poor health which results from it. Expenditure per head in Scotland is higher because successive Governments, under the British system, have produced conditions under which a large part of the population are living in poverty and poor housing. Overall Government revenue and expenditure is a very different matter. The tendency of British Governments has always been to concentrate expenditure in London and the South East of England.

The existence of the European Union makes independence easier to achieve because it removes any possibility of a restriction of the market or of freedom of movement. It is the final answer to the old scare stories about customs posts on the border. At the same time, the European Union makes independence more necessary and more urgent. Europe now legislates on matters which affect almost all

aspects of our lives, including many which are within the functions
of even a devolved Scottish Parliament. We shall be at a hopeless
disadvantage without the right to participate in the process of
European decision making and without the right to have our views
and interests taken into account. On the other hand, the European
Union will increasingly take over functions now exercised by
Westminster. The European currency is likely to be followed by
European defence and foreign policy. Westminster will increasingly
become the superfluous level of government, and a troublesome
interruption between the matters best settled at a European level
and those at a national level in Edinburgh.

The independent Scotland of the past was very closely involved
with Continental Europe to our mutual benefit. The consequences
are still evident in our law, literature, architecture and ideas. Andrew
Fletcher of Saltoun struggled to preserve Scottish independence at
the time of the Union and he was also an advocate, much in advance ˌ
of his time, of European co-operation. In his *Scotland:A New History*
Michael Lynch said that the adoption by the Scottish National Party
in the late 1980s of a policy of independence in Europe "re-establishes
one of the most important threads of continuity in Scottish history."[13]
It seems to me that every rational consideration points to that as the
policy which Scotland should now follow.

References

1   H J Hanham, *Scottish Nationalism,* (London 1969), pp98,113.

2   R J Finlay in *Scotland in the 20th Century*, ed. T M Devine and R J Finlay (Edinburgh 1996), p70.

3   R J Finlay, *Independent and Free* (Edinburgh 1994), p20.

4   Such as, for example, Sir Regind Coupland, *Welsh and Scottish Nationalism,* (London 1954); H J Hanham, *Scottish Nationalism.* (London 1969); Jack Brand, *The National Movement in Scotland,* (London 1978); R J Finlay, *Independent and Free,* (Edinburgh 1994) and a *A Partnership for Good?* (Edinburgh 1997); Alice Brown, David McCrone and Lindsay Paterson, *Politics and Society in Scotland,* (London 1996); Alan Clements, Kenny Farquharson and Kirsty Wark, *Restless Nation,* (Edinburgh 1996).

5   Clements, Farquharson and Wark. *op. cit.*, p67.

6   *Ibid.* p67.

7   Phillipe C. Schmitter and Johan Olsen in *The Future of the Nation State*, ed. Sverker Gustavsson and Leif Lewin, (London 1996), pp215,216,274,275.

8   See Chapter 4 above.

9   Paul Schulter in *Analysis*, BBC Radio 4, 19th September 1991.

10 Garret Fitzgerald in *The Irish Times*, 13th July 1991.

11 Mary Robinson, interview in *The Scotsman*, 29th June 1992.

12 Emile Noel, *Scotland on Sunday*, 5th March 1989 and *The Scotsman*, 12th June 1989.

13 Michael Lynch, *Scotland: A New History*, (London 1991), ppxx, xxi.

CHAPTER 8

Conclusion

The purpose of the Union from the English point of view was to secure their northern border by so controlling Scotland politically that it could never again enter into an alliance with France. Scottish intentions hardly came into the matter because both parties to the negotiation were appointed and controlled by the English government. After the consequences of a century of only semi-independence since 1603, Scotland was in a very weak bargaining position and the Scottish commissioners felt powerless to resist. The Treaty still had to be made acceptable to a majority in the Scottish Parliament against the very clear opposition of the great majority of the Scottish people. This was achieved by the inclusion of articles in the Treaty which appealed to the self interest of the groups represented in Parliament by straightforward bribery and by the implied threat that the alternative was an English invasion and the imposition of worse terms.

As Ruth Wishart wrote recently, "the Union was a thinly disguised takeover,"[1] an arrangement dictated by a stronger country and imposed on one which was not only smaller and weaker, but was then in a particularly vulnerable condition. That does not necessarily mean that all the consequences of the Union were bad for Scotland. Human actions tend to have unforeseen consequences, as the literati of the Scottish Enlightenment were fond of pointing out.

From the English point of view, the Union was one of the most successful acts of statesmanship in their history. Apart from the Jacobite incursion of 1745, the Union permanently neutralised Scotland as a military threat. It meant that England could pursue its imperial ambitions and its continental war against France without having to keep a wary eye to the north. Scotland was not only neutralised, but incorporated as a market, a source of tax revenue and of men for the army and navy. A pamphlet at the time said: "England secures an old and dangerous enemy to be their Friend, and thereby Peace at home and more safety to carry on Designs Abroad."[2] Scotland was described by Daniel Defoe as an "inexhaustible Treasure of men."[3] A little later and more cynically General Wolfe, the conqueror of Quebec, said of the Highlanders: "they are hardy, intrepid, accustomed to a rough country, and no great mischief if they fall."[4]

Advantages to Scotland are less obvious. In the 19th century many Scots, perhaps the majority, thought that the Empire justified the Union. For some industries it provided a captive, or at least privileged market and source of raw materials. It offered an outlet for Scottish energies and provided careers for administrators, explorers, soldiers, engineers, teachers, doctors, missionaries and so forth and provided a high proportion of the generals and colonial governors, and eventually leaders of the independence movements. Many Scots felt that partnership in the Empire was engagement in a great philanthropic mission which spread Christianity and civilisation. Although Scotland became for a time a substantial industrial power, the country itself showed signs of the absence of a responsible government. Standards of health and housing were poor; poverty was widespread; millions of people were lost through emigration.

Scotland was a partner in colonisation, but it was also exploited in a way similar to colonisation at its worst. The Empire could hardly have been established, administered or defended without the help of the Scots, many of whom paid with their lives. Scotland also contributed to the British Exchequer through taxation, but there was very little government expenditure in Scotland itself. Richard Finlay wrote recently: "In 1868, for example, at the zenith of British global economic power, Scotland contributed over 16% to the British Exchequer and got next to nothing back, most going to London, Ireland and the Empire."[5] The highly inequitable treatment of Scotland financially was one of the causes of the increasing agitation for Home Rule in the second half of the 19th century.

Since the middle of that century it has been customary to argue that the Union brought economic advantages to Scotland because it gave access to the English and colonial markets. Such advantage as there was varied at different times and with different commodities; but it is not all certain that Scotland benefited over all and in the long run. To quote Richard Finlay again: "The Union was never really an economic construct and political economy and Unionism do not go hand in hand. Indeed, they are bad for one another. The more Unionists go on about the economic dangers of nationalism the more they undermine their free market position. The message is confused and contradictory."[8]

Possibly the best way to judge whether the Union has benefited or harmed Scotland is to compare the present state of the country with that of countries of a comparable size and situation which have retained or recovered independence, say the Netherlands, Austria, Switzerland or the Scandinavian countries. They are not only more prosperous than Scotland but evidently more content and more at ease with their place in the world. When Sir John Sinclair introduced the *Statistical Account of Scotland* in the 18th century, he said that its purpose was to ascertain "the quantum of happiness enjoyed by its inhabitants, and the means of its future improvement."[7] Happiness cannot be measured like the GNP, but it is, after all, what matters most because it shows the total effect of all the factors which affect the quality of life. Can we judge what have been the effects of the Union on the "quantum of happiness"? What have been its psychological, social and cultural effects? Scotland is a small country which has made a contribution to science and the arts and to civilisation generally which is out of all proportion to its size. You might expect the Scots to draw from this both confidence and a spur to emulation. In fact, you find among a large section of the Scottish population precisely the opposite, a crippling inferiority complex. In his book, *Out of History*, Cairns Craig says: "Scottish culture has cowered in the consciousness of its own inadequacy, recognising the achievements of individual Scots simply as proof of the failure of the culture as a whole ... And the consequences of accepting ourselves as parochial has been a profound self-hatred."[8]

These are strong and disturbing words. That it is possible for a sympathetic and well-informed Scottish academic to speak of contemporary Scotland in these terms shows that there is something fundamentally wrong with the state of the country. And Craig is not alone. I have already quoted C. G. Watson who spoke of finding in Scotland: "the sense of weariness, of the absence of hope, of lacerating self-contempt which is a marked component in the psyche of colonised peoples." [9] And Eric Linklater: "People degenerate when they lose control of their own affairs."[10]

William Wolfe has suggested that psychological problems of this kind are due to a repressed sense of shame over the way in which the Union was brought about.[11] I do not doubt that such feelings were involved in the intellectual contortions of the 18th century and perhaps with some people they linger still. Dependence and political subordination, the mere absence of control, are likely to lead to a sense of resentment and inferiority. Much of Scottish education has tended in the same direction, and more recently so has broadcasting, by their strong Anglo-centric bias. This has given the impression that Scotland is a back-water where nothing important ever happens. Scots have been made to feel ashamed of their own languages and that in speech and everything else they should try to imitate the English. In his recent book, *The Identity of the Scottish Nation,* William Ferguson frequently remarks on the habit of some English historians and critics to deride and belittle everything Scottish.[12] This curious habit has persisted from the 12th century to the present and has been adopted by some Anglicised Scots. These attacks have probably contributed to the loss of Scottish self-confidence, especially as they usually come from the centre of power and prestige in or near London.

These psychological effects of the Union have, I think, been of far more importance than any economic consequences. They are very damaging and increasingly so because of the increased intervention in our affairs of both government and broadcasting from London. To some extent we were protected in the past by our *de facto* autonomy, but this has been eroded by modern communications and more active government. Our political subordination has been particularly harmful because just as our economy is very different from the English so too are our intellectual attitudes and values. The 19th century English historian, H. T. Buckle, made a long study of this matter in preparation for his *History of Civilisation*. His conclusion was that there was an "essential antagonism" between English and the Scottish minds:

> An antagonism extremely remarkable, when found among nations, both of whom, besides being antiguous, and constantly mixing together, speak the same language, read the same books, belong to the same empire, and possess the same interests, and yet are, in many important respects, as different, as if there had never been any means of their influencing each other, and as if they had never had anything in common.[13]

This difference means, I think, that the Union has deprived us of the opportunity of evolving a form of society which suits us. We have at times had to tolerate Governments with which we profoundly disagreed. We have been made to feel dependent impotent and frustrated. For many people this has had the psychological consequences which Cairns Craig has described. If we can shape our own society, one which reflects our instincts and values, it should be one in which we can find the satisfaction at present denied to us and help to restore our self-confidence. It might also become an example to others, just as our education, philosophy, science and technology have been in the past. The restoration of even a limited Parliament will enable us to begin this process, but it is inadequate. The humiliation of dependence will continue as long as our Parliament is subject to the financial control and vast range of the powers reserved to Westminster. We shall still have no real international identity, and no opportunity to enjoy the full benefits of membership of the international organisations, especially the European Union, until we return to normality and resume independence.

Fortunately, our national culture and identity is, as Ferguson says, "remarkably tough and resilient."[14] It has survived all the discouragements to which it has been subjected and has been experiencing a fairly continuous revival since the 1880s. For the reasons which I have mentioned, awareness of this has, in the past, been confined to a minority; but it is now wide-spread. We are evolving in way which is consistent with tendencies throughout the world. On the one hand, empires and multi-national states are dissolving into their component parts, and at the same time international co-operation is increasing. Similarly, there is pressure through the global economy and instant communication towards world-wide uniformity, but in compensation smaller cultures are reasserting themselves.

Those who resist Scottish independence like to call it separatism, but it is in fact the opposite. It means the return of Scotland to full participation in the rest of the world. As in the past, it means that we shall be able to cultivate and benefit from our relations with the rest of Europe. This includes England with whom our relations will also improve because we shall no longer suffer from the frustration and resentment that follow from subordination.

Everywhere else in the world the recovery or the achievement of independence has brought a great increase of self-confidence and creative energy, the "quantum of happiness" in fact. Scotland has never lost the basic structure and memory of statehood and is better equipped to resume responsibility for itself than most of the scores of other states which have become independent in the last fifty years.

Independence will enable us to reach our full potential and, in a phrase used by the founders of the Saltire Society, restore us to our proper place as a creative force in European civilisation.

References

1   Ruth Wishart, in *The Herald*, 6th July 1998.

2   An anonymous Pamphlet, possibly by William Seton, *Scotland's great Advantages by a Union with England*, (1706).

3   Daniel Defoe, *An Essay At Removing National Prejudices Against A Union with Scotland*, Part I, (London 1706), p8.

4   General James Wolfe, quoted in Robert Wright, *Life of Wolfe*, (London 1864), pp168-9.

5   Richard J Finlay, *Scotland on Sunday*, 19th July 1998.

6   *Ibid.*

7   Sir John Sinclair, *quoted* in Alexander Broadie, *The Scottish Enlightenment An Anthology,* (Edinburgh 1997), p558.

8   Cairns Craig, *Out of History*, (Edinburgh 1996), pp11,12.

9   C J Watson, 'The Novels of Neil Gunn' in *Literature of the North,* ed. David Hewitt and Michael Spiller (Aberdeen 1983), p140.

10   Eric Linklater, *The Lion and the Unicorn*, (London 1935), p26.

11   William Wolfe, in an interview with George Byatt, *A Look at the Scottish Psyche*, privately printed, September 1992.

12   William Ferguson, *The Identity of the Scottish Nation* (Edinburgh 1998), pp151,157,227.

13   Henry Thomas Buckle, '*On Scotland and the Scotch Intellect*' in *History of Civilisation*, (1857 and 1861), ed. H. J. Hanham, (Chicago 1970), p395.

14   Ferguson, *op. cit*, p316.

Books for further reading

The best one volume history of Scotland is Michael Lynch's *Scotland A New History* (Century 1991 and paperback Pimlico 1992). William Ferguson's *Scotland's Relations with England* (John Donald 1977 and paperback Saltire Society 1994) is an excellent account of the relationship between the two countries from the earliest times to 1707.

Andrew Fletcher and the Treaty of Union by Paul H. Scott (John Donald 1992 and paperback Saltire Society 1994) deals in some detail with the debates in the Scottish Parliament and the other events which led to the Treaty. The fullest account from an English point of view is P.W. J. Riley's *Union of England and Scotland* (Manchester University Press 1978). The best contemporary account and one of the livliest historical memoirs in our literature is George Lockhart of Carnwath's *Memoirs of the Union*. A modern edition was published in 1995 by the Association for Scottish Literary Studies (ASLS) as *Scotland's Ruine*, edited by Daniel Szechi. There have been two recent editions of Andrew Fletcher of Saltoun's *Political Writings*. David Daiches edited one for the ASLS in 1979. The other edited by John Robertson with a rather misleading introduction, was published by Cambridge University Press in 1997. The most recent edition of Sir Walter Scott's *Letters of Malachi Malagrowther*, edited by Paul H. Scott, was published by Blackwoods in 1981. Extracts from Fletcher, Scott and other relevant documents, including the full text of the 1707 Treaty, are included in *Scotland: An Unwon Cause*, with the same editor (Canongate 1997).

The effects of the Union are, of course, discussed in the general histories of Scotland since 1707. Among the very few books specifically on this subject are: *The Union of 1707: Its Impact on Scotland*, edited by T. I. Rae (Blackie 1974); *Scotland Since 1707: The Rise of an Industrial Society* by R. H. Campbell (second edition, John Donald, 1985); and *Scotland and the United Kingdom: The Economy of the Union in the Twentieth Century* (Manchester University Press 1995). There is much relevant comment in *Exploring the Scottish Past* by T. M. Devine (Tuckwell 1995) and *Image and Identity* edited by Dauvit Broun and others (John Donald 1998)

Conditions in contemporary Scotand are described in *Anatomy of Scotland*, edited by Magnus Linklater and Robert Denniston (Chambers 1992), and *Scotland in the 20th Century*, edited by T. M. Devine and R. J. Finlay. (Edinburgh University Press 1996).

Some Other Saltire Publications

About the Saltire Society

The Saltire Society was founded in 1936 at a time when many of the distinctive features of Scotland's culture seemed in jeopardy. Over the years its members, who have included many of Scotland's most distinguished scholars and creative artists, have fought to preserve and present our cultural heritage so that Scotland might once again be a creative force in European civilisation. As well as publishing books the Society makes a number of national awards for excellence in fields as diverse as housing design, historical publication and scientific research. The Society has no political affiliation and welcomes as members all who share its aims. Further information from The Administrator, The Saltire Society, 9 Fountain Close, 22 High Street, Edinburgh. EH1 1TF Telephone 0131 556 1836.